BETWEEN fRIENDS
❖ Quilts to share ❖

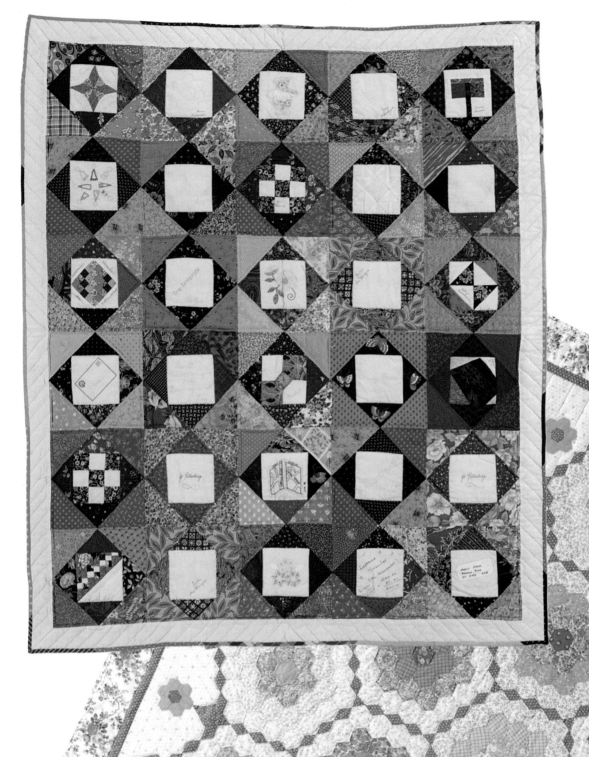

BETWEEN fRIENDS
❖ Quilts to share ❖

KAREN FAIL

CONTENTS

INTRODUCTION

One of my very favourite quilts is on the front cover of this book. It is my friendship quilt from The Quilters' Guild of Australia. Each block was made by someone I know well – someone I had worked with while on the committee of The Quilters' Guild from 1990 to 1993.

At the end of my time as president, I was presented with this wonderful quilt. Knowing my busy schedule, the committee had not only sewn the blocks together, but basted the quilt ready for quilting. What an overwhelming gift! It is a constant reminder, not only of the exciting time I had working for the Guild, but of the people who shared my enthusiasm for quilting and became my friends. I will always treasure it.

This was not my first friendship quilt. Years before I had started a friendship group with members of The Eastwood Patchwork Quilters. Intrigued with the stories about friendship quilts in the nineteenth century, we began with great zeal and, by the end of the year, had made twelve stunning quilts. There were still over fifteen quilts to make and mine was one of them. It was hard to be patient. My 'Homespun Ocean Waves' quilt was finally made and, as it was one of the first really scrappy quilts I owned, I love it. Having quilted with this group for some time, I can identify the maker of each block by the fabric used, even though the blocks weren't signed.

There seems to be a certain mystique associated with the making of a friendship quilt. Often this making is done in secret and everyone involved becomes quite conspiratorial. The anticipated pleasure in the giving seems to become an overriding factor, as other projects are put aside and finishing the block on time becomes all important.

My enthusiasm for friendship quilts has not diminished, even though I have been participating in friendship groups for nearly ten years. I continue to revel in the creativity and pleasure that is generated in designing and executing these memory-filled quilts. This book is full of wonderful stories of friends and their quilts, from the very traditional Album block quilt to the outrageous 'Friendly Fungi' quilt. Be inspired!

FRIENDSHIP QUILTS

THE CRAFT REVIVAL

In today's fast-moving society, many of the traditional roles of men and women have been put aside in the Western world. Gone is the stereotypical image of the male as the provider and the woman as the homemaker. Since the Second World War, when women joined the workforce and performed many roles usually reserved for men, change has been inevitable. These days, it is not unusual for women to run their own companies or become engineers, while increasing numbers of men join the nursing profession or become at-home dads.

While welcoming the opportunities that come from being freed from traditional constraints, and recognising that people are more free to make decisions about their lives, the need to interact with other women is still keenly felt by many women. This need has, in part, led to a worldwide revival of interest in the traditional crafts.

For both the career-minded woman and the at-home mother, the chance to be creative as well as cognitive is treasured, and the opportunity to care and share is welcomed in the learning environment. Heirloom sewing, folk art, embroidery and patchwork are all enjoying this unprecedented revival, along with many other crafts. Skills that were once used to make clothes and household items out of necessity are now being learned and used to create heirlooms of the future. Designs developed to camouflage poor-quality furniture today are used to create treasured folk art pieces. Patchwork quilts are made lovingly from carefully selected pieces purchased from specialty patchwork shops, rather than from the fabric in the scrap bag. It seems that women without a traditional family support network and the everyday interaction in a neighbourhood have found ways of establishing similar structures that offer opportunities for creativity and friendship. Craft groups and guilds have sprung up everywhere, providing camaraderie, instruction and the opportunity for 'show and tell' through exhibitions and meetings. The proverbial 'pat on the back' is, of course, an essential part of the creative process.

Quiltmaking has always been recognised as an interactive craft, with a high level of sharing between the participants. Born out of necessity, when quilts provided warmth for many families during the bitter winters in frontier America, quiltmaking encompasses many inviting images. Perhaps it is the very nature of the quilt as a bed cover that conveys feelings of family, closeness, caring and warmth. With this ever-present need for women to provide bed coverings for their families and the drive to create something of beauty in a harsh environment, there were always quilts to be quilted on the frontier. Today, it is difficult for us to imagine the deprivation suffered by women and their children in the

FRIENDLY FANS, *169 cm x 190 cm, 1995.*
Made by Epping Patchwork Quilters for Elaine Gallen

pioneering West, housed in an earth-lined dugout with a draughty roof over their heads, far from family and friends. Their collection of quilts offered them some measure of warmth, both physical and emotional.

'Back when I was a girl, quilts were something that a family had to have. It takes a whole lot of cover to keep warm in one of them old open houses on the plains.' (Patricia Cooper and Norma Bradley Buferd, *The Quilters – Women and Domestic Art, An Oral History*, Anchor Press/Doubleday USA 1978.)

Great excitement greeted the completion of a quilt top. Women in the area would anticipate a quilting bee and wait for their invitation to participate. They would travel considerable distances to be part of a 'bee' and often these events would create an opportunity for new neighbours to be introduced for the first time. While these events were ostensibly to complete the quilting of the quilt, the real benefits for all those who gathered were found in the enjoyment of each other's company, the sharing of hopes and dreams for the future and a time to relax, away from the harsh realities of their daily lives. Such was the popularity of these events that, when the quilting was finished, the men were invited to join the women for a shared meal and to be part of the fun.

Young women in America were all taught to piece blocks from a very early age, while girls in Australia were working on cross stitch samplers. Sometimes, the lessons in piecing began when a daughter was as young as four. Simple triangular and square shapes were assembled to form the block patterns, and the running stitch required for stitching was demonstrated and corrected when necessary. Often at quilting bees, the younger girls were allowed to thread the needles so there was a continual supply of thread for the quilters. Everyone appreciated the necessity of these skills and young women would aim at completing at least twelve quilts in anticipation of their marriage. After marriage, many new wives travelled to isolated areas in the West with their husbands. Their quilts, packed in a trunk, were an essential part of their luggage.

DESPITE THE NEED FOR WARMTH IN THESE DESOLATE AREAS, SOME QUILTS REMAINED CAREFULLY FOLDED AT

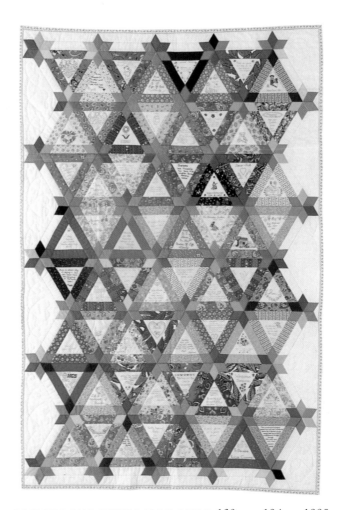

DENISE'S SMOOTHING IRON QUILT, *130 cm x 194 cm, 1995. Made by friends and family for Denise East*

THE BOTTOM OF THE TRUNK AND WERE RARELY, IF EVER, USED. THESE WERE FRIENDSHIP QUILTS. KEPT IN NEAR-PRISTINE CONDITION, THEY WERE A CONSTANT REMINDER OF FAMILY AND FRIENDS WITH THEIR MESSAGES OF LOVE AND FRIENDSHIP WRITTEN CAREFULLY ON EACH BLOCK.

Thousands of friendship quilts were made in America during the nineteenth century, especially from 1840 to 1878. As families moved from the settled villages in the New England area into the newly established frontier towns, the idea of friendship quilts went with them. Simple blocks, pieced from scraps, were soon being made by many women throughout the country. In fact, some of these women would have had their name on several friendship quilts. Friendship blocks were usually of a simple design, not unlike those used for everyday quilts. More often than not, these quilts had a light coloured piece in the centre so that the maker

DETAIL OF 'MY FRIENDSHIP QUILT', *150 cm x 180 cm, 1993.*
Made by friends for Lillian Atkinson

DETAIL OF ALBUM QUILT, *170 cm x 225 cm, 1987.*
Made by friends for Annette McTavish

could sign her name and write a greeting. A popular choice of pattern was the Album block (above left and right).

There were several ways a friendship quilt could be made. One way, was to send the pattern for the proposed friendship quilt to various family members and friends in the hope that they would make a block from their scraps. Each woman considered it essential to have a scrap bag in which every piece of fabric was saved, because new cloth was expensive and considered a luxury. In the scrap bag would be offcuts from past dressmaking, household linen and furnishings projects, and these would be selected to be included in the friendship block. The blocks would then be returned, either signed or with the maker's name attached. Sometimes, one person with a particularly attractive copperplate handwriting was chosen to write the name of each maker on their block.

Friendship quilts could also be made by only one person from fabric she collected from her family members and friends.

LINDA OTTO LIPSETT IN HER BOOK *REMEMBER ME* (THE QUILT DIGEST PRESS, 1985) DESCRIBES LUCY BLOWER'S FRIENDSHIP QUILT AS A COLLECTION OF BLOCKS MADE BY LUCY OVER MANY MONTHS FROM FABRIC SUPPLIED BY HER FRIENDS AND FAMILY FROM THE MATERIAL OF THEIR FAVOURITE DRESS. LUCY IS REPORTED TO BE PARTICULARLY FOND OF HER QUILT AS SHE WAS ABLE TO PICTURE THE PEOPLE SHE LOVED IN THEIR FAVOURITE OUTFITS.

Sometimes, the maker would only require her family and friends to sign their names to a block, after she had completed all the blocks herself.

During the 1830s and 1840s, the autograph album was extremely popular in America, with friendship being romanticised by such publications as *Godey's Lady's Book*. Poems and thoughts suitable for inclusion in these treasured albums were often included in Godey's, and it was not long before these began to appear on friendship quilts. It was also during the 1830s that indelible inks, made from a mixture of silver nitrate, ammonia and lampblack, had been developed in France, making the process of writing on fabric an attractive alternative to painstakingly embroidering signatures. Previously, the only inks available contained iron which rotted fabric and left a nasty stain. Simple messages like 'Remember Me' or a verse from a favourite poem could now be included, along with the maker's signature. Often, the signatures were hidden among elaborate drawings of scrolls, tiny leaves and flowers. Such was the enthusiasm for these ornate inscriptions on friendship quilts, that stamps and stencils of them were soon developed, with a space in the centre for name signing to make this type of embellishment easier.

Commonly, a friendship quilt was presented to a woman by her family, when she was leaving to make a new life with her husband, or by a community where she had lived for some time. Any event, in fact, could be the stimulus for making a friendship quilt, from births and weddings to leaving for the mission field.

Because these quilts were so treasured, many have survived and provide a lasting record of the inhabitants of a town or the people who made the quilt. Even the names of deceased family members were often included. In some circumstances, these quilts are the only record of the female members of a family as, sadly, the government records only listed the heads of families – usually men.

THE *RAJAH* QUILT

Working together on quilts was not the sole prerogative of the American quilter. As early as 1841, the convict women bound for Australia aboard the *Rajah*, worked on a quilt for Elizabeth Fry. She and her Quaker committee, as part of their prison reform measures, had been providing an

REPRODUCED BY PERMISSION OF THE NATIONAL GALLERY, CANBERRA

RAJAH QUILT, *325 cm x 327 cm, 1841.*
Made by the women aboard the Rajah *for Elizabeth Fry*

opportunity for gainful employment for women from Newgate Prison. These hapless women were given materials for sewing and knitting and were then able to sell the finished items. These measures were very successful and led to Mrs Fry's decision to provide fabric and sewing supplies to the women being sent to the colony in New South Wales. The British Society of Ladies, as Mrs Fry's organisation became known, gave each reluctant traveller a Bible; one hessian apron; one black stuff ditto (bag); one black cotton cap; one large hessian bag; one small bag, containing one piece of tape, one ounce of pins, one hundred needles, four balls of white sewing cotton, one ditto black, one ditto blue, one ditto red, two balls of black worsted, twenty-four hanks of coloured thread, one cloth with eight darning needles, one small bodkin, two stay laces, one thimble, one pair of scissors, one pair of spectacles, two pounds of patchwork pieces, one comb, one knife and fork. With these supplies, it was anticipated that the women would make quilts

REVEREND NADAL'S QUILT, *260 cm square, 1847.*
Made by parishioners and friends for Reverend Bernard Nadal

in the traditional English style, so they would have something to sell at the end of their horrific voyage.

The level of skill among the women who worked on the medallion quilt for Mrs Fry was very varied, and little care was taken to see that exactly the same-sized templates were used or that borders finished in an appropriate spot. It is obvious that many hands worked on the quilt, as the borders change along their length, as does the size of the shapes and their accuracy. Nevertheless, the quilt is quite complex – an accomplishment for those women living in such cramped conditions on board the *Rajah*. Preserving every bit of precious fabric they had, they appliquéd small motifs onto the central square, using the broderie perse technique so popular in England at that time. Surrounding it is a quite complex border of pieced squares and triangles. The final wide border has more broderie perse and appliqué.

Although not signed by each individual who shared in the work, the quilt does bear the following inscription:

'To the ladies of the Convict Ship Committee this quilt worked by the Convicts of the Ship Rajah during their voyage to Van Diemans Land is presented as a testimony of the gratitude with which they remember their exertions for their welfare while in England and during their passage and also as a proof that they have not neglected the Ladies kind admonitions of being industrious. June 1841.'

On receiving the quilt, Elizabeth Fry must have felt that her work with the women prisoners was not in vain, and surely it would have become one of her most treasured possessions.

The women from the *Rajah* do not appear to have maintained their enthusiasm beyond this one medallion quilt, and they failed to embrace Elizabeth Fry's suggestion that quiltmaking could be a viable cottage industry in the developing town of Sydney. Lack of initiative, as well as the extremely poor supply of fabric in the colony, certainly would have contributed to this situation.

WHILE THERE WERE MANY FRIENDSHIP QUILTS MADE IN AMERICA USING SIMPLE GEOMETRIC PATTERNS, SOME QUILTS WERE MORE ELABORATE AND INVOLVED QUITE COMPLEX APPLIQUE BLOCKS. THESE WERE KNOWN AS ALBUM QUILTS, THE MOST FAMOUS OF WHICH WERE THE BALTIMORE ALBUM QUILTS.

It is thought that these superbly executed appliqué designs were the work of a few talented women, like Mary Evans of Baltimore, who completed blocks on commission from wealthy women of the area. These wonderful quilts were often given to those held in very high esteem. Not all appliqué friendship quilts were as elaborate or meticulously worked as the Baltimore Album quilts, but appliqué was often chosen to create very special quilts. A much-loved travelling pastor might be the recipient of a special appliqué quilt from the women of the circuit, who usually made only serviceable quilts for their families.

'We sent out the word by him along the circuit for ladies of other congregations to send a design for the top. He could carry them little appliquéd

pieces easy in saddlebags, no weight to 'em. We gathered it all in and put that quilt together. That was a feat in those days. He said he never seen anything so pretty. It was a treasure.' (Patricia Cooper and Norma Bradley Buferd, *The Quilters — Women and Domestic Art, An Oral History*, Anchor Press/Doubleday USA 1978.)

Perhaps this quilt was like the one presented to the Reverend Bernard H. Nadal of Baltimore. His quilt top reflected the trend for complex appliquéd blocks to be included in friendship quilts, if the person receiving the quilt was held in high regard. Most of the blocks have embroidered or inked details, with the red Bible, dated 1847, in the centre square inscribed 'To Rev. Bernard H. Nadal, Baltimore'. Nearly all the inscriptions appear to have been done by the same hand, demonstrating the trend to employ a single person with a good standard of copperplate writing to inscribe all the names and messages. This quilt top is in the collection of the Smithsonian Institution in the United States, a gift of Miss Constance Dawson, great-niece of the Reverend Bernard Nadal.

By 1870, after the Civil War, America was recovering economically and women wanted the freedom to buy, rather than make their bed linen. Although quilts were still being made, the making of friendship quilts became less fashionable. Indeed, the use of cotton fabrics was considered passé. With the introduction of velvets and silks for clothing, these fabrics quickly replaced cotton in quiltmaking, and crazy patchwork became the fad. Australian women usually kept up with the trends overseas and, by 1890, many of them were experimenting with crazy patchwork and the use of silks and satins in traditional quiltmaking. The making of friendship quilts was one trend that was not observably followed in Australia at this time. The quilts made during 1830 to 1870 were in the English style of quiltmaking, using one shape, such as the hexagon, or medallion-style like the *Rajah* quilt. In the early part of the nineteenth century, these quilts were made in cotton, but by 1890, quilts using hexagon and diamond shapes were fashioned in the richer silks and satins now readily available in the colonies.

AUNT CLARA'S QUILT (Above), *150 cm x 200 cm, 1915;*
Clara Bate as a young woman (Top Right);
DETAIL OF 'AUNT CLARA'S QUILT' (Right)

Aunt Clara's Quilt is a remarkable Australian quilt which emulates the style of crazy patchwork with its ornate embroidery stitches, but features a black square surrounded by a regular elongated hexagon as the basic unit, rather than irregularly shaped pieces. It is reminiscent of a pattern recorded in Caulfield's *Dictionary of Needlework* in 1887. The hexagons are cut from a variety of exotic fabrics of many hues, including some plaids and stripes, among the mostly plain fabrics. Each hexagon is embroidered with a symbol of everyday life, including garden tools, vegetables and flowers, garden bugs and spiders, pipes, firecrackers, a telephone, dates and names: the list is endless. Many different techniques and styles of embroidery are used, including satin stitch, French knots and feather stitch. Various trinkets, like clay pipes and tiny handbags, were attached to the quilt and are still preserved, a testimony to the care given to the quilt by the present owners. The quilt was completed in 1915, the last date recorded on the quilt. Family folklore suggests that the quilt is like a diary, recording the daily events in Clara Bate's life, and the comings and goings at her guesthouse, Frankfurt, at Gingkin, New South Wales at the turn of the century. One story, passed down through the family, concerns the recurring pipe motif on the quilt. While travelling on a train, a passenger accused Clara of giving him hayfever and promptly threw her offending flowers out of the window. She retaliated by snatching his pipe out of his mouth and tossing it from the train, complaining of the smell.

The variety of styles of embroidery on the quilt suggest that many hands participated in its making. Perhaps Clara invited her guests to contribute and this is, in fact, her friendship quilt, a reminder of all the interesting people who visited her guesthouse. The quilt was completed by Clara's sister, Emma, during 1915, after Clara's death on 18 December 1914.

CHANGI QUILTS

The elegance and excellence of Aunt Clara's Quilt is in direct contrast to the simple embroidered quilts known as the Changi quilts. After the surrender of Singapore to the Japanese on 15 February 1942, many soldiers and civilians were interned in camps at Changi on Singapore Island. Over three thousand men, women and children were crowded into a facility originally designed for six hundred people, the women arriving by foot with whatever possessions they could carry. It was essential that the women be able to communicate with their husbands in the military camps. Ethel Mulvany, who had worked for the Red Cross, suggested that they make quilts embroidered with their own names and other motifs as a means of letting the men know they were safe.

In the early days of the camp, there were limited supplies for sewing, which some of the women had managed to bring with them – despite their hasty departure from their homes.

ON THE WHITE FABRIC SQUARES THAT WERE DISTRIBUTED, EACH WOMAN EMBROIDERED HER NAME AND SOMETHING ABOUT HERSELF. WONDERFUL IMAGES WERE CREATED WITH LIMITED RESOURCES AND THERE WERE EVEN ATTEMPTS AT HUMOUR, WITH ONE BLOCK READING 'CHANGI HOLIDAY HOME'. THE BLOCKS WERE THEN SEWN TOGETHER BY MACHINE AND THE SEAMS EMBROIDERED.

While these quilts are not typical friendship quilts, they were made with the same spirit of communicating love and care to others. Three quilts are still in existence, although it is thought that several more may have been made. These three were each made from sixty-six squares, and each had an inscription on the back. One was for wounded Australian soldiers, one for the English soldiers and one for the Japanese soldiers. The inscription on the quilt for the Australian soldiers reads:

'Presented by the women of Changi Internment Camp 1942 to the wounded Australian soldiers with our sympathy for their suffering. It is our wish that on cessation of hostilities, this quilt be presented to the Australian Red Cross Society. It is advisable to dryclean this quilt.'

The women hoped that when the quilts were presented to the hospital in the military camp, the men would be encouraged by the patriotic messages. They thought that including a quilt with an inscription for the Japanese soldiers would improve the chances of the other quilts arriving at their chosen destination. On arrival, the names on the quilt were quickly circulated throughout the camp, reassuring many that their wives and children were safe and well. Two of the three surviving quilts are housed at the Australian War Memorial in Canberra, and the third at the Red Cross Training Centre at Barnet Hill, England.

CHANGI QUILT, *130 cm x 203 cm, 1942.*
Made by the internees of Changi POW camp

FRIENDSHIP QUILTS, *160 cm x 220 cm, 1965.*
Made by Ilma Hinwood

AUSTRALIAN FRIENDSHIP QUILTS

Before the revival of quiltmaking in the 1970s, first in America and eventually worldwide, the quilts made in Australia continued in the English tradition. Many of these quilts, made during the first half of the twentieth century, were traditional hexagon quilts. Construction was quite different from the American system where pieces were sewn together using a running stitch. Here, each shape was basted to an exact paper hexagon before the pieces were whipstitched together. When the top was completed, the basting was removed along with the papers.

It is unusual to find an Australian quilter who followed American traditions and patterns during that time; however, one such quilter was Ilma Hinwood, now aged eighty-six, who took up quiltmaking in the 1920s. Greatly influenced by the quilts being made in America, she made twin quilts for her husband and herself. As one set wore, she would make another, completing several pairs of quilts for their twin beds. Favouring appliqué, Ilma chose such interesting themes as wedding customs

around the world, and scenes from Louisa May Alcott's book, *Little Women*. She also made two friendship quilts during the early 1960s. Ilma asked family members and friends to embroider or write their name on the small squares of fabric she provided, then she appliquéd these around the central panel of her quilts, which feature flowers and birds arranged slightly differently for each quilt. Her daughter-in-law, Marilyn Hinwood, remembers using the quilts when she visited her mother-in-law. Ilma was not interested in her quilts just being showpieces. She was always keen for her quilts to be used.

FOLLOWING THE RESURGENCE OF INTEREST IN QUILTMAKING IN AMERICA IN THE 1970s, AUSTRALIAN QUILTMAKERS QUICKLY FOLLOWED SUIT, ADJUSTING TO THE NEW TECHNIQUE OF PIECING WITHOUT PAPERS AND WELCOMING THE WIDE RANGE OF TRADITIONAL PATTERNS ON OFFER.

Some Australians, like Heather Madden of Epping, New South Wales, were lucky enough to be living in America during this time. Heather joined a newly formed quilting group, called the Trumbull Piecemakers, while living in Connecticut. When she was about to return to Australia in 1978, the group presented her with a friendship quilt. It features simple pieced and appliquéd blocks joined with cream and brown sashing, and each block is signed. One of the blocks shows a map of the United States marked with the location of the Trumbull Piecemakers.

Tiny Kennedy, from Launceston in Tasmania, is an expatriate American who is the proud owner of a friendship quilt from her friends of the Gabilian Mountain Quilters in San Juan, California. Tiny designed her own house block and each one of the group of twelve picked a month of the year and decorated the house block with that month in mind. Some houses are decorated for Christmas and Thanksgiving, while others welcome spring and summer. Tiny was so thrilled by her blocks that she decided to make a rainbow of triangles as a border. This was all before half-square triangles and quick-piecing had been thought of! 'Friends across the Sea' was completed in time for the first Tasmanian Quilters' Guild's Exhibition in 1984. With many adjustments to be made in a new country, Tiny found her quilt a constant reminder of her friends back in America.

Quilts, like Heather's and Tiny's were made in the tradition of friendship quilts where several friends each made a block and signed it, as a memento for a friend who was leaving. Sometimes, the person receiving the quilt was surprised and delighted with this special gift, as was Heather, but often they were completely involved in the making of the quilt, just like Tiny, who actually designed the block and distributed the instructions for its completion.

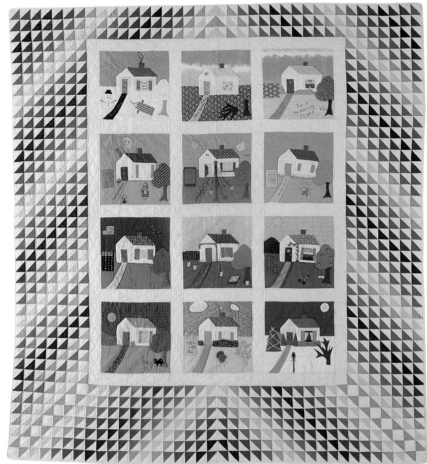

MY AMERICAN EXPERIENCE (Above Right), *180 cm x 230 cm, 1978.*
Made by the Trumbull Piecemakers for Heather Madden

FRIENDS ACROSS THE SEA (Right), *248 cm x 255 cm, 1984.*
Made by the Gabilian Mountain Quilters for Tiny Kennedy

As enthusiasm for quiltmaking grew in Australia, so did the making of friendship quilts. Quilters began to form small groups to make each other friendship quilts. Usually, the names of group members were placed in a container and drawn out in turn to determine the order of the making. Then, each member of the friendship group, when it was her turn, would decide on a pattern for her block and perhaps a colour scheme and, within a month, the completed blocks would be returned to her.

In some groups, the package handed out also included the templates and any background fabric that the owner wanted to remain consistent. Other groups preferred to cut out the entire block, then all that was required was for the participants to sew them. Participants were usually asked to sign their blocks and some were even asked to embroider motifs and their names on the completed blocks, such as on Sylvia Fenech's quilt pictured opposite.

These early friendship quilts reflected the basic, simple style of quiltmaking. However, with more experience, the planning of the quilts became quite sophisticated, demonstrating interesting settings, original block designs and clever coordination.

The Western Australian Quilters' Association was formed in 1981 and the idea of friendship quilts rapidly gained acceptance among its members. Faye Cunningham's hat quilt was planned so that each hat would reveal something about the maker. One hat even has a feather from the quilter's budgie attached to it! Faye says the quilt reminds her of the times when she and her friends used to travel to town in hat and gloves. With four of the participants now in their eighties and some having returned to live in America and England, this quilt is one of Fay's treasured possessions.

News about quilts, exhibitions, group activities, workshops and tutors was easily disseminated, once the quilters' guilds were formed in each state. The enthusiasm for friendship groups and the quilts they made was contagious. Groups all over the country set in place the processes for making friendship quilts. These same processes were used to make quilts for charity, following the generous example of quilters of the past.

One Sydney group, the Eastwood Patchwork Quilters, embraced with great gusto the idea of making friendship quilts and, even though they had nearly twenty members, decided to form a friendship group in 1985. As you can imagine, there was a long wait for some, but for those whose name was drawn giving them an early slot, there was great excitement. The first name drawn was Evelyn Finnan's, who chose a scrappy 'Autumn Breeze' quilt from a pattern in the *Quilter's Newsletter*. It was a frantic time for Evelyn, as she only had one month to work out her design and prepare more than twenty packs of instructions. The rules were simple: choose a block with less than twenty-four pieces

FOURTEEN FRIENDS FRIENDSHIP QUILT, *147 cm square, 1983.*
Made by the Western Australian Quilters' Association for Faye Cunningham

and provide any templates required and any fabric you want to be consistent in the blocks. The pattern sheet, instructions for making, together with prepared templates and fabric, if required, were packaged and given to each member of the group. Evelyn's design involved two different blocks, so she divided the members into two groups, with each one completing a different block. She provided cream homespun with the templates already marked on the fabric and asked her friends to provide autumn-toned fabrics for the leaves.

THE ADVANTAGE OF WORKING WITH A LARGE GROUP IS THAT YOU RECEIVE LOTS OF BLOCKS; THE DISADVANTAGE IS THAT IT CAN TAKE A LONG TIME FOR YOUR TURN TO COME AROUND, IF YOU ARE UNLUCKY ENOUGH TO BE DRAWN LAST. MOST GROUPS EVENTUALLY CONCEDE THAT TWELVE MEMBERS IS THE OPTIMUM SIZE, AS EVERYONE RECEIVES THEIR BLOCKS WITHIN A YEAR.

After the initial round of friendship quilts was completed, the Eastwood Patchwork Quilters broke into smaller groups, each with twelve members. One group decided to be a challenge group for those who wanted to tackle harder blocks. Jo Petherbridge of Asquith chose Feathered Stars for her challenge friendship block and requested that the blocks be machine-pieced. To obtain the accuracy required, using the machine, was indeed a challenge for everyone involved, but the resulting quilt was spectacular. The challenge enabled many of the group to refine their machine-piecing skills, and Jo was always available with helpful advice.

FEATHERED STARS (Top Right),
165 cm x 225 cm, 1991.
Made by the Eastwood Patchwork
Quilters for Jo Petherbridge
AUTUMN BREEZE (Centre Right),
205 cm x 256 cm, 1985.
Made by the Eastwood Patchwork
Quilters for Evelyn Finnan
FRIENDSHIP RINGS (Right),
238 cm x 262 cm, 1995.
Made by the Castle Hill Quilters for
Sylvia Fenech

USE OF SIMPLE BLOCKS

Traditionally, very simple blocks were chosen for friendship quilts and the Album block, a favourite in the nineteenth century, is still a popular choice. Annette McTavish of Beecroft, New South Wales, has a beautiful Album block quilt, inscribed with names and messages from the members of her group, Just Friends. This group was initially formed to make friendship quilts and has made over one hundred quilts since the group's inception in 1983. Annette's friends chose not to write on the blocks, preferring to embroider their messages instead.

Moon over the Mountain is such a simple block that it is rarely chosen by

GRANDMOTHER'S FLOWER GARDEN (Above), *204 cm x 360 cm, 1933.*
Made by the Northbridge Quilters for Anne Docker
ALBUM QUILT (Left), *170 cm x 225 cm, 1987.*
Made by American friends for Annette McTavish

quilters, even in a beginner's sampler quilt. But Faye Cunningham's quilt, made by members of the Quilters' Network, is a delight. Quilters' Network is organised by Marti Johnson, who lives in Sacramento, California, and communicates with quilters worldwide through a quarterly newsletter. Member quilters from Brazil, Japan, Hungary, Ireland, Norway, Belgium, America, Canada and Australia make 'cuddle' quilts for quilters in trouble, and have fabric and block exchanges. When Faye participated in a Moon over the Mountain block exchange, she never dreamed that she would win the blocks. When she did win, Faye wondered how she could make an interesting quilt from what she thought were uninspiring blocks. Her idea of adding 'stars and details like the witch on a broomstick, has certainly worked and now she treasures her international friendship quilt, made by quilters from America, Canada, England, Austria, New Zealand and Australia.

Anne Docker from Northbridge, New South Wales, chose Grandmother's Flower Garden for her friendship block, using a simple hexagon template.

HER LOCAL GROUP, THE NORTHBRIDGE QUILTERS, HAD DECIDED THAT EVERYTHING HAD TO BE CUT OUT READY FOR SEWING FOR THEIR FRIENDSHIP QUILTS. WHILE IT SEEMED AN ONEROUS TASK TO CUT OUT OVER ONE THOUSAND HEXAGONS, IT WAS EVEN MORE ONEROUS TO CONTEMPLATE SEWING THEM, SO ANNE WELCOMED THE OPPORTUNITY TO HAVE A HEXAGON FRIENDSHIP QUILT.

When she received the completed blocks, Anne realised she had been too liberal with the hot pink fabric. In an effort to tone this down, she added the green diamonds when setting the blocks together. Starting with a simple block, Anne has created a majestic quilt.

Another very simple block design is Mayflower. Mayflower is a very welcome choice for those making friendship blocks, because it is so easy. Helen Sears of Eastwood, New South Wales, received a delightful selection of fabrics when she asked for a scrappy Mayflower block quilt. To maintain uniformity, Helen provided the background fabric which she then quilted heavily to create her beautiful quilt.

INTERNATIONAL MOONS (Top Right),
152 cm x 205 cm, 1992.
Made by the Quilters' Network for Faye Cunningham
MAYFLOWER (Right), *180 cm x 210 cm, 1990.*
Made by Eastwood Patchwork Quilters for Helen Sears

UNUSUAL SETTINGS

Even the simplest block can look stunning, when the blocks are set in an interesting way and the finished quilt is heavily quilted. Margaret Scott of Epping, New South Wales, set her simple Crosses and Losses blocks, made in various shades of blue, in a medallion style which allowed generous spaces between the blocks. With such a nautical feel to the quilt, Margaret decided to use sailing ships as the quilting motif, which she quilted beautifully in the large triangles surrounding her central medallion of blocks. A member of her group has a husband in the Navy — his books on sailing ships provided the quilting patterns. Margaret says she really appreciated the input from several members of her group on both the setting of the blocks and her quilting design.

Small groups need not be a bar to generously sized friendship quilts. With only eight members in her group, Bearly There Quilters of Hornsby, New South Wales, Judy Ellis had to make an extra twenty-four blocks herself to complete her beautiful 'Path to Granny Sullivan's House' quilt. The use of two tones of green to set the blocks creates an interesting effect, with fourteen of the blocks set into a dark green border. Judy has lived most of her life in the country, in the little town of Merriwa in the Hunter Valley and has only recently moved to Sydney. As a result, being part of the Bearly There Quilters has special significance for her, creating an instant circle of friends with common interests. When Judy received her friendship blocks, she embroidered each person's name on their block, giving her a constant reminder of their friendship to a 'girl from the bush'. The quilt has pride of place on her bed.

Most friendship blocks are of uniform size, but when there is no size restriction, interesting dilemmas are created for setting the blocks.

The idea for Lauree Brown's friendship quilt came to her as she was recovering from a fractured elbow, spending much of her time sitting at her living room window, gazing at the sky and the view over Launceston, Tasmania. In an effort to capture that image of the night sky, she asked her friends to make any star, comet or planet pattern, using cottons or shiny chintz fabric in red, pink, orange, gold, yellow, white or

SAIL ON (Above),
65 cm square, 1994.
Made by the Eastwood
Patchwork Quilters for
Margaret Scott

silver, patterned or plain fabric from their scrap bags. Lauree provided the blue background fabric. Each person was invited to embroider her name on the star, comet or planet in a contrasting colour.

Lauree assembled the blocks so that they looked like the night sky, using the blue background fabric she had supplied to join the blocks and fill in the gaps. She then applied a black silhouette of gum trees and the outline of the surrounding hills, festooned with sequins, beading and embroidery to represent the

lights in the valley. The hand-quilting was completed in 1991. Lauree called her unusual friendship quilt 'Friends Remind Me of the Stars in Heaven' and feels it is a fitting reminder of so many wonderful friends.

PATH TO GRANNY SULLIVAN'S HOUSE (Above Right), *185 cm x 238 cm, 1995.*
Made by the Bearly There Quilters for Judy Ellis
FRIENDS REMIND ME OF THE STARS IN HEAVEN (Right), *217 cm x 226 cm , 1991.*
Made by the Launceston Quilters for Lauree Brown

AN AUSTRALIAN IDENTITY

In the 1980s, Margaret Rolfe and Deborah Brearley began to develop an Australian identity for quiltmaking by publishing original designs featuring Australian wildflowers and animals. These designs proved very popular and many Australian quilters incorporated them into quilts and clothing, especially for children. Occasionally, these designs are chosen for friendship quilts, creating charming quilts which are recognisably Australian.

Margaret Parry from Epping, New South Wales, has made a small quilt, featuring Deborah Brearley's wattle pattern. The pattern is very simple, using only a square in yellow and white to give the impression of Australia's national floral emblem. Margaret provided all the fabrics for the blocks and asked each of the members of Epping Quilters to sign their names in white or yellow thread. This ensured that her friends' names were included on her quilt, without detracting from the design. She arranged the twelve blocks to create a delightful medallion-like centre, with half the wattle pattern being used to create the border. Margaret used a thick wadding and simple quilting, in keeping with the puff of yellow wattle.

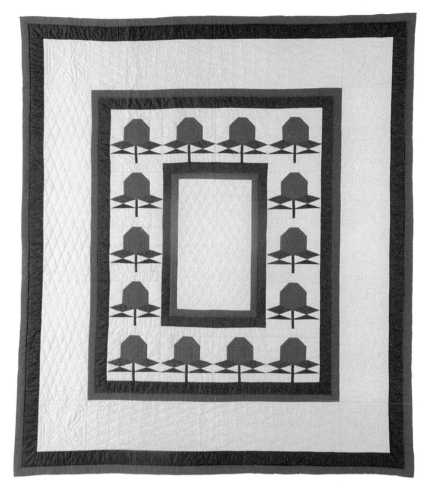

WARATAHS (Above), *232 cm x 265 cm, 1994.*
Made by the Marion Quilters for Dot Foster
WARATAH CUSHION (Below Left)

THE BOTTLEBRUSH, ANOTHER ORIGINAL BLOCK DESIGN BY DEBORAH BREARLEY, IS FEATURED IN THE FRIENDSHIP QUILT MADE FOR SANDRA JAMES BY THE EASTWOOD PATCHWORK QUILTERS. THE BOTTLEBRUSH BLOCK USES ONLY A SIMPLE RECTANGULAR SHAPE, AND SANDRA'S FRIENDS HAVE INTERPRETED THE FLOWER EFFECTIVELY BY USING INTERESTING PRINTS AND COLOURS THAT REFLECT THE FEATURES OF THE FLOWER.

With twenty-eight blocks to include in her quilt, Sandra chose a very successful symmetrical placement, adding detailed quilting of the bottlebrush in the blank squares. The whole design is unified by the green fabric Sandra has chosen for the blank blocks, reminiscent of the foliage of the bottlebrush bush.

The Marion Quilters made Waratah blocks for Dot Forster from Clovelly Park, South Australia. Dot comes from England, and she chose this design

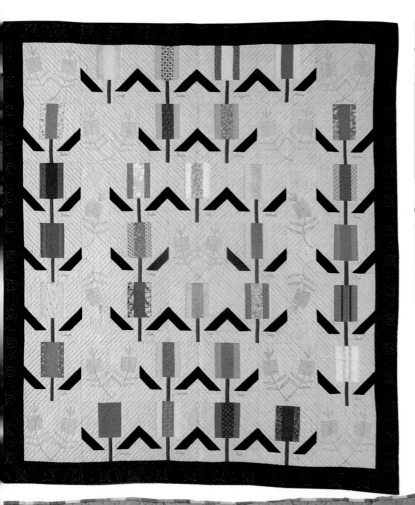

as she wanted a truly Australian quilt. She was also keen to provide all the fabrics for each block, as she had very definite ideas about how she wanted her quilt to look. She arranged fourteen of her fifteen blocks around a rectangular central panel to create a very graphic quilt, which she then quilted beautifully with a grid pattern. The fifteenth block was made into a cushion, on which are recorded the names of all the participants, in the order of the placement of the Waratah blocks in the quilt. Rather than putting the names on the back of the quilt, as other members of her group had done, Dot wanted them on display, and her treasured cushion is always on the brass bed which was bought especially to display Dot's wonderful waratah quilt.

BOTTLEBRUSH BOUQUET (Above Left), *200 cm x 230 cm, 1995.*
Made by the Eastwood Patchwork Quilters for Sandra James
DETAIL FROM 'BOTTLEBRUSH BOUQUET' (Top)
WATTLE QUILT (Left), *140 cm x 147 cm, 1995.*
Made by the Epping Quilters for Margaret Parry

CUT-OUTS

Many quilters like the variety and the surprises that come when friends are asked to use their own fabrics for friendship blocks. However, some quilters like to engineer their quilts so that they receive blocks for a specific quilt. Heather Wootton asked her friends at the Eastwood Patchwork Quilters to piece all the baskets she needed to make her basket quilt. Each of the sixteen participants received identical fabrics, already cut out with the seam lines marked, ready for hand- or machine-piecing. When the completed blocks were returned, Heather decided to add appliquéd flowers and leaves on the basket handles.

WITH THE HELP OF A FELLOW EASTWOOD QUILTER, STEPHANIE INTRONA, SHE DESIGNED SOME DELIGHTFUL FLOWERS ENTWINED AROUND THE HANDLE AND REPEATED THE MOTIFS ON THE LARGE CALICO BORDERS. WHEN HEATHER HAD FINISHED CROSS-HATCHING THE ENTIRE QUILT USING A TWO-AND-A-HALF CENTIMETRE GRID, SHE HAD HER DREAM QUILT.

The Northbridge Quilters of New South Wales always provide cut-outs for their members — each block cut out and ready for sewing. For Robyn King's beautiful 'Fox and Geese' quilt, all twenty-eight blocks were pieced by her quilting friends, from fabric supplied and cut out by Robyn. When the blocks were pieced, she set them on point with plain blocks in between and bordered them with Flying Geese. Providing cut-outs for friends to sew together is proving very popular in today's busy society. With the invention of self-healing cutting boards and rotary cutters, together with specially marked rulers, the process of cutting pieces for an entire

FOX AND GEESE (Top), *142 cm x 243 cm, 1994.*
Made by the Northbridge Quilters for Robyn King
BASKETS OF FLOWERS (Above), *225 cm square.*
Made by the Northbridge Quilters for Heather Wootton

quilt is very quick. The Northbridge Quilters find that it takes no time at all to machine the pieces together for their friendship blocks, ensuring that they all get at least one quilt top each year from their friendship group.

Another member of Northbridge Quilters created a very scrappy quilt, still using the cut-out method. While her quilt does not have recognisable pieces from other people's fabric stashes, Sheelagh Thompson loves her scrappy variation on a nine-patch, using her collection of blue and red fabrics with touches of yellow. Using the blue check as the unifying fabric, Sheelagh has created a charming small quilt, machine-quilted in a simple design.

As part of the 1988 Bicentennial celebrations, the Castle Hill Friendship Quilters decided to make every member of the group a 1988 friendship quilt. This was quite an ambitious goal, as there were twenty-four members in the group at the time. One of them, Viive Howe, drew up a roster for the handing out and returning of blocks and, to speed things along, the group decided to provide cut-outs for everyone. Each person added some embellishment or embroidery to their block to give it a personal touch. Angela Langdon, now of Carseldine, Queensland, was involved in this project and decided to choose North Carolina Lily for her block. She handed out kits, containing the cut-out pieces for the block, the pattern and the complete instructions. Angela also included a triangle of Aida cloth on which each member was invited to embroider their name. When the block was assembled, the Aida cloth triangle formed the basket for the lily. The quilt, which Angela now has on her bed, holds many memories of the friendships she made while she was a member of the Friendship Quilters of Castle Hill, New South Wales.

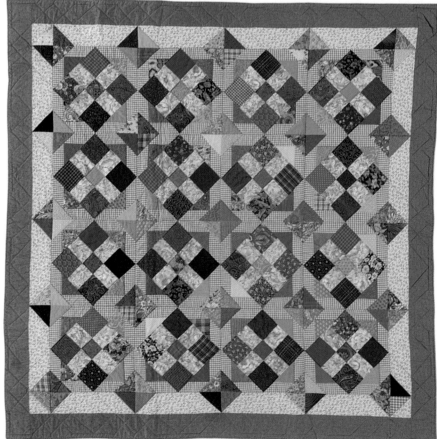

NORTH CAROLINA LILY (Top), *228 cm x 276 cm, 1992.*
Made by the Castle Hill Friendship Quilters for Angela Langdon
SCRAPPY NINE-PATCH (Above), *150 cm square, 1994.*
Made by the Northbridge Quilters for Sheelagh Thompson

HOME SWEET HOME, *127 cm x 190 cm, 1992.*
Made by the McLaren Vale Quilters for Pam Waite

RECURRING THEMES

The strong link of quilts with hearth and home might go some way to explaining the popularity of the house as a theme for friendship quilts. Marlene Boatwright of Launceston, Tasmania, has a spectacular house quilt made for her by the Launceston Patchworkers and Quilters. Her love of house blocks led her to make this her choice for a friendship quilt. Friends were free to do anything they liked – as long as the blocks were 30 cm

(12 in) square and used the blue fabric Marlene supplied for the sky. New skills, such as broderie perse and embroidery, were learned as her friends exercised their creativity. Inspiration for the houses came from many sources, including a National Trust publication, *Tasmanian Midlands*. It took three years for all the blocks to be returned!

EACH BLOCK TELLS A STORY ABOUT ITS MAKER – SOME HAVE WONDERFUL FLOWER GARDENS, OTHERS HAVE QUILTS ON CLOTHESLINES. THE FINISHED QUILT IS HUGE, BUT MARLENE SAID SHE COULDN'T LEAVE ANYONE OUT AND IT WAS WORTH THE WAIT! MARLENE HAS WRITTEN THE NAMES OF ALL HER FRIENDS ON THE BACK OF THE QUILT IN A DELIGHTFUL HOUSE LABEL.

Pam Waite from McLaren Vale, South Australia, also wanted a house theme for her friendship quilt, but she asked for the houses to be set against anything but a blue sky. The variety and uniqueness of her collection of house blocks is typical of the McLaren Vale Quilters. Originally a group of spinners, these ladies decided to make quilts for each other, and now do very little spinning and lots of patchwork! For their friendship quilts, they nominate a theme, which is often just one word – for example, houses, chooks or clowns. The size of the block is not necessarily specified, creating interesting dilemmas when it comes to setting the blocks. Appliqué is often used to interpret the given theme and this is true for Pam's houses with only a few traditionally pieced house blocks evident. To finish her quilt, Pam has added a wonderfully zany border to her collection of zany houses.

Marion Russell of Angaston in South Australia decided to set her house friendship blocks into a house of the same design. Marion is a 'member by post' of her friendship group, which is based in an area approximately two hours away from her home. Marion sent her fifteen prepared blocks to the other members of the group by mail, but she planned to be present at the meeting when the blocks were returned. As she had provided and cut out all the fabrics, she hoped that the group members would add their own personalities to the blocks with their decorations and embellishments. Marion travelled to Victor Harbor to collect her blocks and to meet all the people who had made them. She was delighted with the results – each house is very individual, with the addition of all sorts of embellishments, such as flowers, cats, chooks, spiders and webs, curtains and beautiful front doors. Marion calls her quilt 'House Proud', because she is very proud of her quilt.

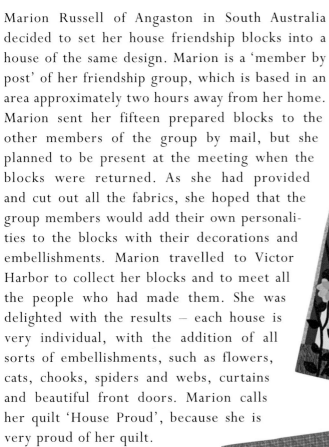

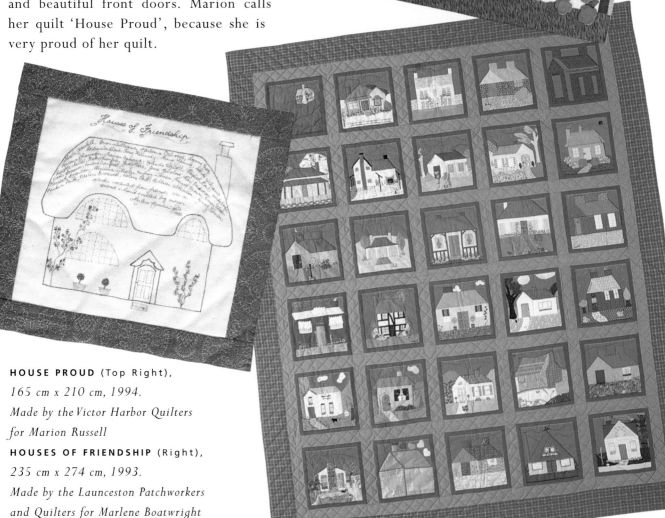

HOUSE PROUD (Top Right),
165 cm x 210 cm, 1994.
Made by the Victor Harbor Quilters
for Marion Russell
HOUSES OF FRIENDSHIP (Right),
235 cm x 274 cm, 1993.
Made by the Launceston Patchworkers
and Quilters for Marlene Boatwright
DETAIL OF THE LABEL FOR 'HOUSES
OF FRIENDSHIP' (Above)

Cats are another recurring theme for friendship quilts. For her 'paper bag' quilt, Yvonne Wooden, another of the McLaren Vale Quilters, chose the theme of 'Cool Cats'. Paper bag friendship quilts are a new idea for friendship groups. Yvonne decided on the theme, created the background for her small quilt, and then put it into a paper bag. Each member of her group did the same with their own quilt design. These bags were then passed around the group, according to a predetermined order, without the originator being aware of what each person had added to her quilt.

WHEN ALL THE 'COOL CATS' WERE ADDED TO YVONNE'S QUILT, AND ALL THE OTHER QUILTS WERE FINISHED, A SPECIAL DAY WAS HELD FOR THE UNVEILING. EVERYONE SHRIEKED WITH DELIGHT AS THE FINISHED QUILTS WERE DISPLAYED TO REVEAL MANY WONDERFUL AND ORIGINAL DESIGNS, LIKE YVONNE'S 'COOL CATS'.

Doreen Carter, although not an inveterate cat lover, also chose cats as her theme for her friendship quilt, to be made by the Marion Quilters. Having just come through a rather difficult period, Doreen decided she wanted to have some fun with her friendship blocks and create a humorous quilt. She borrowed the charming cat illustrations from a quilting friend who had found them in 'some old magazine'. Doreen passed out several different outlines of cats with the instruction: 'Do what you like'. Every cat was different, even those with the same outline. Some even reflected the maker's personality, giving everyone a lot of fun – just as Doreen had hoped it would. She made the corner blocks, and added a butterfly and other embellishments, here or there, to add to the whimsy. The quilt now resides on her bed and, while it is not the usual type of quilt chosen for a master bedroom, it is well used and continues to delight its owner with its variety and sense of fun.

Glenda Olesen of Roleystone in Western Australia was the coordinator of the Western Australian Quilters' Association Bicentennial Quilt Exhibition during 1988. The organising committee had so much fun working together that they decided to form a friendship group, affectionately known as

The '88s. After the first round, when fairly traditional blocks were chosen, the group decided to continue making friendship quilts, but this time to make fun quilts. Glenda chose cats as her theme, providing each member with the Attic Window block with a latticed windowpane. She asked each member to appliqué a cat on the window ledge. When the blocks were completed, a delightful array of pussycats greeted Glenda, including Guy Wackie, the grey cat with its paw hanging down, a combined effort by mother Ngaire (who painted it) and daughter Pippa (who sewed it).

FANTASTIC CATS (Opposite),
153 cm x 223 cm, 1994.
Made by The '88s for Glenda Oleson
COOL CATS CHALLENGE (Above Right),
58 cm x 62 cm, 1993.
Made by the McLaren Vale Quilters
for Yvonne Wooden
CAT-O-LOGUE (Right),
184 cm x 210 cm, 1992.
Made by the Marion Quilters for
Doreen Carter

UNUSUAL THEMES

Quilters must spend a lot of time talking over cups of tea or coffee, judging by the number of friendship quilts using this theme. Barb West of McLaren Vale collects teapots, so she had an additional reason to choose teapots as the theme for her friendship wallhanging. In true McLaren Vale Quilters' style, each member produced a unique teapot, using their own innovative design. Three of the designs are based on work by Clarice Cliff, one on an antique bronze pot, and one was designed from a black metal Japanese teapot given to Joan Harnett (one of the group) by a Japanese friend. The teapots were then appliquéd to different-sized rectangular blocks, leaving Barb with the difficult task of assembling them. Black-eyed Susan from Barb's garden completes the jigsaw of blocks. She has chosen an unusual fabric to border the colourful blocks, which have been outlined in black, giving a stained-glass effect. The typed label on the back of the quilt records all these details, and also includes a photocopy of the 'perfect' teapot, more than one hundred and thirty-five years old which holds sixty-one litres of tea and stands seventy-six centimetres tall. It is presently owned by Twinings. Barb has also included on the label a list of what to look for when buying a teapot and how to clean it.

TEAPOTS (Above), *87 cm x 112 cm, 1991.*
Made by the McLaren Vale Quilters for Barb West
FREE RANGE CHOOKS (Below Left), *153 cm x 196 cm, 1995.*
Made by the Bennethaus Patchers for Bev Bennett

The Bennethaus Patchers of Lane Cove, New South Wales, not only make friendship blocks for the members, but they then go on to finish the quilt. Bev Bennett is the lucky owner of 'Free Range Choox'. She delights in the collection of hens and roosters — and they all have names!

DURING ONE HILARIOUS MEETING OF THE GROUP, THE 'CHOOX' BECAME DRIBBLE AND DRABBLE (THE TWINS), DAFFY, HENNY PENNY, ESTER, CELESTE, STICKY BEAK, LABELIA

(THE VEGETARIAN IN THE COOP), DOIDLE, POLLY, SUZANNAH, DOTTY AND POSH BETTY. RANDY ROOSTER, NAPOLEON AND FLAUBERT ARE THE COCKS. CHICKEN WIRE HAS BEEN QUILTED BEHIND THE STYLISED CHICKENS TO CREATE A CHARMING QUILT, AN ADAPTATION OF A PATTERN FROM THE *RED WAGON* SERIES.

The McLaren Vale Quilters continually come up with wonderful and out-landish ideas for their quilts. Inez Ewers asked the group for a quilt with a food theme – with wonderful results. The whole group was very excited about this theme, and the members were keen to try their hands at something beyond the usual flowers and birds. One member was so enthu-siastic about Inez's plan to give the completed quilt to her daughter, who owns a popular local restaurant, that she decided to use the restaurant logo for her design. Her block has pride of place in the centre of the quilt. Inez called the quilt 'Posh Food' and now the completed quilt, adorned with all good things to eat, hangs in the restaurant, where it is quite a talking point.

Not daunted by the task ahead of her, Emma Wood, the daughter of one of the McLaren Vale Quilters, joined in a friendship round. The blocks she made were of a very high standard for a twelve-year-old and everyone was delighted to make her a clown block when it was her turn. Emma finished her wonderful quilt herself.

POSH FOOD (Above), *166 cm x 214 cm, 1991.*
Made by the McLaren Vale Quilters for Inez Ewers
CLOWNS (Below), *172 cm square, 1992.*
Made by the McLaren Vale Quilters for Emma Wood

Beryl Hodges, now of Isaacs in the Australian Capital Territory, was one of the members of The '88s in Western Australia. The friendship group started out as an exhibition committee. The members enjoyed each other's company so much, they decided to continue meeting, making a friendship block each month. By the time it was her turn to choose a block, Beryl was living in Sydney and a 'member by post' of the group.

SHE DECIDED THAT AS SHE COULD NO LONGER MEET WITH THE OTHER GROUP MEMBERS PERSONALLY, THEY SHOULD EACH MAKE A BLOCK OF THEIR OWN FACE AS A KEEPSAKE.

THEY WERE ALL HORRIFIED! BERYL RECEIVED SEVERAL OF HER BLOCKS WITH LETTERS ADDRESSED TO 'DEAR EX-FRIEND'! BUT BERYL WAS DELIGHTED WITH THE RESULTS AND IMPRESSED WITH HER FRIENDS' INGENUITY.

One had used fine Vylene to create her glasses, another chose fleece for her fluffy white hair, while a third friend had used brown satin to show Beryl the colour she had recently dyed her hair. One block even arrived unsigned, with a note suggesting that the likeness was so apparent, Beryl should have no trouble identifying the maker. Beryl arranged her blocks to resemble a gallery of portraits,

A STITCH IN TIME, *122 cm square, 1993.*
Made by the Marion Quilters for Mary Jarvis

providing her with a constant reminder of a lovely group of friends.

Mary Jarvis, a member of the Marion Quilters of South Australia, chose clocks as the motif for her quilt. She has a particular interest in clocks, because of her family history. In 1836, some of her ancestors arrived in South Australia aboard the *Buffalo*, along with Governor Hindmarsh, who was to proclaim South Australia a colony. At that time, an uncle, back in England, promised a grandfather clock to each of the four sons in the family on the occasion of their marriage. He honoured his promise and today the location of three of the four clocks is known. Mary's ancestor received the missing fourth clock and she is still trying to track it down. So the theme was a natural choice for Mary's friendship quilt. When her group was first told about the project, they were unsure of their ability to comply. But Mary encouraged everyone by cutting out appropriate photographs of clocks and explained the techniques needed to complete the blocks. The blocks could be funny or traditional. Most of the group chose to create something humorous and Mary made these into a separate wallhanging, which her grandchildren especially enjoy. She added two more blocks, featuring traditional clocks, to her collection from her group to make a second wallhanging. She inscribed on the middle left block the inscription "'Stands the church clock at ten to three, And is there honey still for tea' Rupert Brook". The block had been made by a close friend who had been heard reciting this quote when Mary announced the theme for her friendship quilt. A photograph of the French boudoir clock was sent to Mary by a visiting quilter, who is delighted to have her clock included in Mary's quilt.

DETAIL FROM 'A STITCH IN TIME' (Top)
GALLERY OF FRIENDS (Above), *130 cm x 166 cm, 1990.*
Made by The '88s for Beryl Hodges

TUTORS BROUGHT PEACE TO MY HEART, *138 cm x 213 cm, 1988.*
Made by friends at the Australasian Quilt Symposium for Margie Furness

Wright's contribution, who at the time was president of The Quilters' Guild and had very little time for stitching.

Judy needed the large floor space of Ranelagh House at Robertson to put the quilt together, and found many willing helpers at the Quilters' Guild Retreat, held there in 1994.

WITH OVER FIFTY QUILTERS ENTHUS- IASTICALLY OFFERING ADVICE, JUDY LAID OUT HER EXTENSIVE COLLEC- TION OF BLOCKS ON THE FLOOR. SOME BLOCKS WERE MADE ON THE DAY, AS NEW RECRUITS JOINED IN THE FUN. JUDY HAD A GREAT SELEC- TION OF UNUSUAL BATIKS TO CHOOSE FROM WHEN ASSEMBLING THE SASHING STRIPS, CREATING HER UNIQUE FRIENDSHIP QUILT.

Friendship quilts have always been reminders of people and places and, often, of exciting and difficult times shared. Margie Furness of Parkdale, Victoria, recalls the unexpected gift of her friendship quilt from the Australian and overseas tutors at the Australasian Quilt Symposium in 1988:

'I was looking for something different to add a touch of merriment to the fashion parade. I was to be the compere

Give all your friends a piece of your favourite batik fabric and ask for a friendship block of any size and any design and the result will be something like Judy McDermott's wonderful quilt. The blue batik is the recurring fabric, providing a linking thread between the very different blocks from friends from all over Australia. Along with traditional blocks were blocks designed especially for Judy's quilt, including a wonderful fish on a plate — complete with knife and fork. This was Margaret

and decided that the Australian tutors could dress up and pretend to be football players. Two teams were formed: the Crazy Quilters and the Olpha Cutters. Week One of the symposium saw the Australian tutors (Lessa Seigal, Noreen Dunn, Shirley Gibson, Elizabeth Kennedy, June Lyons, Lorraine Moran, Megan Terry, Judy Turner, Wendy Wright, and Ruth Walter), dressed in white, burst through a huge banner to the tune of 'Up There

LOAVES AND FISHES, *266 cm x 272 cm, 1995.*
Made by friends for Judy McDermott

Cazaly'. Week Two and it was the overseas tutors turn. Valerie Cuthert from New Zealand performed a traditional Maori dance, Carol McClean from Canada performed 'The Snow Bird', while the Americans stole the show with Doreen Speckman, dressed as the Statue of Liberty, with Carol Bryer Fallert and Catherine Anthony holding her train.

Knowing the difficulties I was working under, after a car accident on the day of the parade, the tutors decided to make me a friendship quilt. The Olpha Cutters made the yellow and black blocks, while the Crazy Quilters used all the colours they knew I loved to make blocks typical of their work. Especially dear to me are Noreen Dunn's Bow Tie blocks. The quilt is covered by loops of rouleau, made by Wendy Wright – a reminder of her patience while she tried to teach me the technique. The quilt was really made in friendship and I am honoured that all these terrific tutors found time in their busy schedules to make this humorous, bright, happy quilt top especially for me. It is, and always will be, one of my greatest treasures.'

VICTORIAN LADIES, *173 cm x 206 cm, 1994.*
Made by Fibres and Fabrics for Brigit Nicol

Brigit Nicol of Nambour, Queensland, makes dolls as well as quilts. As a bridal machinist, she particularly enjoys dressing her dolls and enjoys working with lovely fabrics. When she came across the pattern for her quilt, designed by Jean Teal (copyright 1991), she knew it was something she just had to make. It became her choice for her friendship quilt. She gave out the background fabric, the outline of the dress and asked for it to be made in old-fashioned colours. The dress could be changed in any way – so sleeves were changed and bustles added. Some of the members of her friendship group, Fibres and Fabrics, researched the period costumes at the library, so additions of chains at the hem, used to raise the skirt, were added. Brigit was delighted with the finished blocks, very aware that, had she made all the blocks herself, she would never have had such variety. The blocks were decorated with laces, brooches, necklaces, standaway collars, feathers, frills and lovely bead work. When they were assembled, Brigit added the striking border and the quilt now has pride of place on her lounge-room wall, hanging from a shelf which houses her beautifully dressed dolls.

THE ROAD TO THE HOUSE OF A FRIEND IS NEVER LONG,
160 cm x 170 cm, 1993.
Made by Fibres and Fabrics for Derryn Johnson
DETAIL FROM 'THE ROAD TO THE HOUSE OF A FRIEND IS NEVER LONG'

FIBRES AND FABRICS

Fibres and Fabrics from Townsville, Queensland, make fabulous friendship quilts. As with many friendship groups, they have developed a style unique to their group. Because of the diversity of backgrounds of their members, including spinning and weaving, papermaking, knitting and basketmaking, their work is not restricted by the traditional skills of patchwork. Very few restraints are imposed on the makers, resulting in a varied selection of blocks, featuring a broad spectrum of techniques including all areas of creative embroidery, machine-embroidery, surface embellishments, knitting and, of course, all areas of patchwork and quilting. The themes chosen are often unusual, inspiring even greater creativity.

This group of women with such divergent interests meet happily together as Fibres and Fabrics and they have found that the bond of handwork has no age boundaries, with octogenarians interacting happily with young mothers.

For her friendship quilt, Derryn Johnson, the president of the group, asked for an Australian house in any size and using any style of making. She gave each member of the group a linen square and some fabrics in green and the 'bricky' red she liked. Each participant was asked to put something from her own house on her block.

THE KNITTER IN THE GROUP ADDED KNITTED TREES AND SPIDER WEBS TO HER VERANDAH, WHILE BIRTE, WHO IS DANISH, ADDED THE DANISH FLAG. COLLEEN WHO HAS TWINS, CROSS STITCHED TWO BABIES PLAYING IN THE FRONT YARD, WHILE ANOTHER BLOCK HAS AN ACTUAL PHOTO OF THE MAKER'S DOG AT THE WINDOW.

Derryn wanted to add something of herself to the quilt as well, so she cross stitched some of her favourite sayings about friendship and homes in the spaces between the irregularly sized blocks:

'You can't pluck a rose
All fragrant with dew
Without part of the fragrance
Remaining with you.'
and
'A house is made of brick and stone
A home is made of love alone.'

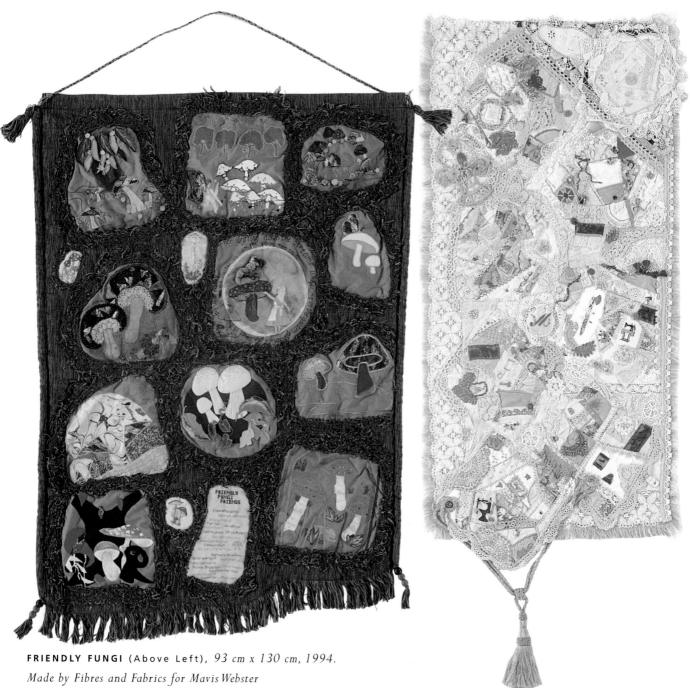

FRIENDLY FUNGI (Above Left), *93 cm x 130 cm, 1994.*
Made by Fibres and Fabrics for Mavis Webster
VICTORIAN CRAZY PATCH (Above Right),
61 cm x 102 cm, 1994.
Made by Fibres and Fabrics for Margaret Wretham

MAUREEN NORMAN, 'FOR SOME UNKNOWN REASON', DECIDED TO ISSUE EVERYONE WITH A RANDOMLY SHAPED PIECE OF BLACK CHINTZ FOR HER QUILT, INVITING THEM TO EMBROIDER A SPIDER'S WEB ON IT. SHE THEN INCORPORATED THE TWENTY-ONE SPIDERS' WEBS INTO HER UNIQUE INTERPRETATION OF A RAINFOREST.

The rainforest surrounding Townsville is often the source of inspiration for Maureen's work and an expression of her concern for its preservation. She says she enjoyed the challenge of the construction, attaching spiders' webs, leaves, ferns and tree trunks to the black background. Maureen employed her considerable skills in dyeing and printing fabric to create the amazing three-dimensional scene, which even includes a painted stream running through it. Machine- and hand-embroidery, couched fibres and fabrics of various textures, such as velvet and leather, were used to complete the extraordinary picture depicted on the quilt.

FRIENDLY SPIDERS, *115 cm x 198 cm, 1995.*
Made by Fibres and Fabrics for Maureen Norman

The 'Friendly Fungi' friendship quilt was the brain-child of Mavis Webster, another member of the amazingly creative Fibres and Fabrics group. She distributed background squares and an evening fabric that was to be incorporated into each block and asked that the group make her blocks depicting mushrooms. The returned blocks featured crazy patchwork, cross stitch, painting, appliqué, knitting and embroidery. Mavis then had the problem of how to put these wonderful blocks together. Eventually, she set them on the back of a piece of textured furnishing fabric, and reverse-appliquéd them into place. Lots of fraying gave an under-growth effect to the whole creation. The sides were finished with covered piping cord, while the bottom was left irregular and frayed. With the blocks she received, Maureen was able to complete two quilts; on one of these, she has included a panel on which she stitched the names of everyone who contributed. 'I will treasure the completed work always,' says Mavis.

Margaret Wretham wanted a Victorian 'Crazy Patch' friendship quilt, because of her love of old fabrics, laces and buttons. Her 'not-so-old' friends lovingly sewed the blocks, using treasured pieces from a grandmother's sewing box, or lace from a great aunt's wedding gown. Margaret assembled the blocks as a merging collage, symbolising the bonds of friendship. The quilt is part of a triptych, but each section can be hung separately.

'Tumbling Friends' is another of the unique quilts created by Fibres and Fabrics. Birte Muller decided to use the traditional Baby Blocks pattern and gave each of her friends a pastel-coloured background fabric and a dark fabric for the darkest side of each cube. The creativity and ingenuity of the returned blocks delighted Birte and she was able to arrange them so the light appears to come from the top left-hand corner as instructed. Birte decided on the octagon shape, which accommodated the seventeen blocks beautifully.

Exotic fabrics, lavish embroidery and embellishments are not usually associated with the Amish, but Barbara Murphy wanted to see how their simple designs and colours blended with the exotic. She supplied the vibrant silk fabrics and some of the beads, ribbons and other embellishments in two colour schemes. Barbara now has 'Byond Amish - Blue' and 'Byond Amish – Red'.

SPECIAL FRIENDSHIP QUILTS

While the majority of friendship quilts are made by friendship groups, where every member eventually receives a collection of blocks to their specifications, occasionally a person or an event inspires the making of a friendship quilt.

During the McLaren Vale Quilters' Retreat, held annually at Douglas Scrub, all the participants make a block to the specifications given. In 1994, the request was for an animal block. Meanwhile, the group had collectively worked a gateway, lettering and people at the zoo, as a background for this unusual quilt. Some of the blocks brought to the retreat were chosen for the quilt and, as at every retreat, Dorothy Fennell secreted herself away

to join the blocks, while the rest of the group enjoyed Saturday night activities. On Sunday morning, all the participant's names went into a draw for the quilt and, to everybody's delight, Dorothy won – a fitting reward for this generous quilter.

TUMBLING FRIENDS (Top Left), *135 cm octagon, 1993.*
Made by Fibres and Fabrics for Birte Muller
DOUGLAS SCRUB RETREAT ZOO QUILT (Left),
147 cm x 196 cm, 1992.
Made by the McLaren Vale Quilters for Dorothy Fennell
BYOND AMISH – BLUE (Above), *102 cm square, 1993.*
Made by Fibres and Fabrics for Barbara Murphy
DETAIL (Right) **FROM 'BYOND AMISH – BLUE'**

FOR ISOLDE II (Top), **FOR ISOLDE I** (Above Right), **FOR ISOLDE III** (Above), *1994.*

Made by the Epping Quilters in memory of Zolda Glockerman

The Epping Quilters have made three wonderful quilts in memory of Zolda Glockerman, a member of the group who died in 1994. Each quilter was asked to make a flower block, using the cream homespun provided as the background. Everyone wanted to participate and thirty-nine finished blocks were received and assembled into three magnificent quilts. Without any planned colour coordination, the blocks naturally fell into three groups, with purple, red and green predominating. One quilt was used as the Epping Quilters' raffle quilt for their open day in October 1995, with the proceeds going to a local charity. A second quilt was handed over to The NSW Cancer Council to use as a fundraiser and the third quilt was given to Zolda's husband, who passed it on to Lifeline, a favourite charity of Zolda's. The generous efforts of the Epping Quilters are reminiscent of the way friendship quilts were made in the past for deserving causes.

Quilters Down Under in Beenleigh, Queensland, make the most of any opportunity to acknowledge one of their members with a special friendship quilt. When May Cook turned eighty in 1993, the

MY EIGHTIETH BIRTHDAY QUILT, *118 cm x 174 cm, 1993.*
Made by Quilters Down Under for May Cook

group members decided to give her a friendship quilt to celebrate the occasion. They chose a simple block, Square in a Square, and used the white centre of each block to record their birthday wishes. While most were content to record a simple message, there is also a scene of a cottage and a cow, a spider's web with the inscription, 'Friendship is hanging around together' and a delightfully decorated M in the centre. There is even a poem, written especially for the occasion:

> 'To marvellous May
> Who just makes our day
> We all miss her terribly
> When she's away.'

MEGAN'S FRIENDSHIP QUILT (Top), *120 cm x 225 cm, 1994.*
Made by the Colours of Australia exhibition subcommittee
for Megan Fisher

COLOURS OF AUSTRALIA *blocks made by the exhibition*
subcommittee for Larraine Scouler (Above)

Often, friendship quilts are made as a lasting acknowledgment of the high regard in which someone is held. The Colours of Australia subcommittee of The Quilters' Guild of New South Wales made just such a friendship quilt for Megan Fisher. Megan had worked very hard as the publicity officer for the committee and had become ill. The instructions were simple: make a Judy in Arabia block, including the deep aqua star points provided. The block could be changed in any way and there was a prize for the most innovative change. (Note the heart block – no sign of a 'Judy in Arabia' block there!) The simple blocks were then set on an angle to add interest. The quilt was presented to Megan, already bound and with minimal machine-quilting – a demonstration of how just a few large blocks can create an interesting quilt.

This subcommittee was responsible for the organisation and implementation of the Colours of Australia touring exhibition and book, recording the collection of forty quilts that will tour Australia until 1999. As a fitting recognition of the work of the chairperson, Larraine Scouler, each of the quilters whose work was selected for the Colours of Australia exhibition, was asked to submit a block reminiscent of their quilt in the collection. Larraine now has a unique collection of blocks from some of Australia's leading quiltmakers which will form a wonderful friendship quilt.

The committee of The Quilters' Guild of New South Wales has generously made friendship blocks for each of their retiring presidents over the last five years. One of those quilts is featured on the front cover of this book. Narelle Grieve, the president from 1990 to 1991 received a quilt top made of small blocks. Each participant had made two blocks that reflected her activity on the committee, a charming reminder for Narelle. The blocks gave some indication of what each person's function was on committee or reminded Narelle of particular incidents during her presidency. Isobel Lancashire embroidered a map on her block, as she always seemed to be navigator for Narelle – often without immediate success in finding their destination.

Quilters often get together to make quilts for charity. Narelle Grieve initiated the making of an

unusual quilt for the NSW Cancer Council for their Posh Auction in 1992. Her quilt was reminiscent of the signature quilts made by the Red Cross to raise money during times of war.

In those days, each participant would pay a small fee for the privilege of signing the quilt. Narelle decided to invite well known Australian sporting personalities to each sign a Snowball block which she then incorporated into a quilt. Of course, she didn't charge them for their generosity! Many hands helped in the making of the quilt. Val Donalson wrote the names on the blocks, so that the signatures could be recognised; Lee Cleland helped assemble the quilt top and Shirley Gibson assisted with the hand-quilting. The quilt was finished in time for the Posh Auction and the successful bid was from The Australian College of Physical Education. The quilt now hangs in the offices of the College at the Sports Centre in Homebush, Sydney, having raised a considerable amount for cancer research.

COMMITTEE MEMORIES (Top), *110 cm x 130 cm, 1991.*
Made by the committee and friends from the Quilters' Guild for Narelle Grieve
SIGNATURE QUILT (Above), *270 cm square, 1992.*
Made by various people for charity
DETAIL OF 'COMMITTEE MEMORIES' (Top Left)

PATRIOTIC GAMES (Above), *165 cm x 210 cm, 1988.*
Made by the Patriotic Quilt Group for Pamela Tawnton
66 STARS LATER (Above Right), *166 cm x 206 cm, 1992.*
Made by Australian and overseas friends for Isobel Lancashire

FRIENDS OVERSEAS

More and more quilters from all over the world are joining forces and making friendship quilts for each other. Those involved say it is an enormous thrill to put a quilt together, knowing that the blocks were made by quilters across the ocean. Isobel Lancashire from Epping, New South Wales, made her quilt '66 Stars Later' with blocks from friends from South Africa and the United States. Several quilters were involved in this project, organised by Dale Ritson and Frances Thurmer in Australia. Each person was asked to make four 30 cm (12 in) star blocks – any star at all. Preferred colours were nominated – Isobel wanted burgundy and pink. She made four blue and cream stars for Marie de Whitt in South Africa and four pink and mauve blocks for Lyn Weigel in the United States. When Isobel received her blocks, she set them on point, alternating her stars with deep blue blocks to create a strong image. The finishing touch was to add sixty-six tiny stars for the delightful border.

Pamela Tawnton of Weston in the Australian Capital Territory joined the Patriotic Quilt Group in Annapolis, Maryland, by default. The group's aim was to make each member a patriotic quilt in the true red, white and blue tradition. Her long-time friend, Jean Pope, offered her a place in the newly formed group and, before Pamela could decide whether to join or not, Jean had said yes on her behalf! Somewhat reluctantly, and wondering how an Aussie would fit in, Pamela agreed to participate. For her quilt, she chose a lovely rust colour for everyone to incorporate into their blocks. 'Patriotic Games' was the result. Her friend Jean added the finishing touch with the Australian flag in the centre. Pamela made the koala block for her own quilt and one each for the eighteen other participants in the group.

THE EXCITEMENT OF BEING INVOLVED WITH QUILTERS FROM OVERSEAS IS SO ATTRACTIVE TO DALE RITSON AND FRANCES THURMER FROM EPPING, NEW SOUTH WALES, THAT THEY HAVE BEEN ACTIVELY INVOLVED IN COUNTLESS PROJECTS SINCE 1986.

Frances' first round of friendship quilts involved two pen friends from the United States – Ruth from Illinois and Kate from Texas – and Stephanie from Berowra, New South Wales. Frances, a passionate letter writer, had made contact with the American quilters through the *Quilters' Newsletter*. For their

CHECKS AND PLAIDS (Above),
170 cm x 180 cm, 1990-92.
Made by Dale Ritson from cut-around blocks
FLIGHT OF FANCY (Above Right),
92 cm x 120 cm, 1992.
Made by Frances Thurmer from cut-around blocks
INVESTMENTS VEST (Below Right), *1995.*
Made by Frances Thurmer

friendship quilts, each participant chose a block pattern and provided templates for each other. Using these, each person cut out four blocks for everyone else. No sewing was required. Everyone agreed to this simple process and loved the idea of receiving parcels from overseas, with blocks cut out ready to sew.

Dale, always keen to be involved in whatever was happening, joined the group for the next round of blocks, when the process was streamlined. A parcel was circulated continually between the members of the group, within a predetermined time-frame. In the parcel was the selected pattern, instructions and templates for each person. When one of the group received the parcel, she cut out a block for everyone else, using the templates provided, and put it into the appropriate envelope. At the same time, she would remove all the blocks cut

out for her and decide whether to continue circulating her current block (if she needed more for her proposed quilt) or change her pattern, instructions and template for a new block design. The parcel was then sent on to the next person. This parcel circulated for several years with these girls becoming firm friends, sharing their family and quilting life through letters and photographs.

The 'cut-arounds' have finally stopped, because Ruth decided she had too many UFOs (unfinished objects) and Kate's husband retired, so she had to go 'cold turkey' and withdraw from the group.

The enthusiasm for working on friendship projects with overseas quilters has not waned for Dale and Frances. They can't wait for their weekly meeting to sew, catch up on the news from overseas friends, and open the latest letter or package.

Even though the original group has disbanded, other friendship groups have been established over the years in Australia, America, South Africa, England and Germany.

At present, they are involved in a round-robin friendship quilt with participants in America, and four charm robin groups with

Guardian Angels

Australian quilters. They also make large progressive quilts with two American quilters, Betty and Tammy, and small progressive quilts with Beth and Alma, from New Jersey in the United States. In addition, Frances is involved in an 'investments' round robin, where each quilter makes part of a vest for the others. As well as their enthusiastic interaction with quilters from overseas, Dale and Frances are involved in making traditional friendship quilts with their group of quilting friends at the Eastwood Patchwork Quilters.

The recent publication of *Round Robin Quilts* by Pat Maixner and Margaret and Donna Ingram-Slusser, has inspired a new type of friendship quilt. Moving away from the traditional set of square blocks, they advocated a completely new look for friendship quilts, using small and large blocks arranged on a grid. Each quilter decides on a theme, and makes a large 20 cm (8 in) or 30 cm (12 in) block that reflects her theme, together with some simple 10 cm (4 in) filler blocks (again reflecting the theme). A 10 cm (4 in) or 5 cm (2 in) grid, is drawn up on Pellon (a very thin wadding), and the completed blocks are pinned into place. Each person in turn adds to the quilt by completing small blocks that fit the chosen

HEAVENS ABOVE (Above), *Work in progress*
QUILT LABEL FROM 'HEAVENS ABOVE' (Right)

MINIATURE SAMPLER QUILT (Above),
47 cm x 51 cm, 1993.
Made by Dale Ritson
DALE'S BLUE RIBBON (Above Right),
Made for her by her friend Rita

theme. The blocks may be any size, as long as they will fit exactly into the grid. For Dale and Frances' group, each participant has to make at least six blocks, two of which are designed around the theme, while the other four are simple, geometric filler blocks. These blocks are then pinned to the grid in a pleasing arrangement, but, of course, the final decisions rest with the owner.

Dale and Frances heard about the round-robin quilts through the *Lucky Block Newsletter* and, of course, they wanted to be part of it. Frances chose for her theme 'Heavens Above' and Dale chose 'Give me a Home among the Gum Trees'. Frances began her quilt with an appliqué angel set in the centre of a brilliant yellow star block. The others added to her 'Heavens Above' quilt with more angels and stars, some appropriate verse and even a sunrise (pictured page 48). As each member of the group completed her blocks, she signed the label that Frances had prepared.

Each participant in the round robin is encouraged to include a quilt label with their instructions, so everyone can write their name and address on it as a permanent record of those involved. This is attached to the back of the finished quilt. Many round robin-members also include a journal in their parcel. The journal encourages the bonds of friendship, as it is passed from one quilter to the next, with each person recording their thoughts about the quilt, adding fabric samples, photos, and news of family and quilt happenings.

The *Lucky Block Newsletter*, to which Dale and Frances subscribe, is produced by Patricia Koehner in America. All those who register their interest send Patricia a block they have made, following the instructions in the newsletter. The blocks are then divided up into piles of twenty and one block is selected from each pile. Those selected win all the blocks in their pile. The newsletter, a quarterly publication, is also used to convey all sorts of information to its international readership, and it was here that Dale and Frances not only learned about round-robin friendship quilts, but they were introduced to Betty from Idaho and Tammy from Wyoming, and the Toledo sisters – two from Arizona and one from Mexico. They all decided to make a large progressive quilt for each other. Each participant was required to make a 40 cm (16 in) block, which was then passed on in turn to the others who were required to add borders of specified widths. Each person tried to reflect the original block when completing their borders. Frances drew up the entire border with a little help from her engineering husband, while Dale just began and worked towards the middle of each border, then used her creativity to ensure absolute accuracy. No one in the group saw their quilt top until it was completed a year later.

STAR SAMPLER, 150 cm x 226 cm, 1992.
Blocks made by Rita for Dale Ritson

Dale recently made a wonderful miniature sampler quilt. As she made each tiny block, she made a second identical block and sent it to Rita. Dale assembled them, using little strips of Liberty prints. To add the finishing touch to her quilt, Rita attached some of the charms Dale had been enclosing in her letters. Rita's quilt won a blue ribbon at her local quilt show, so she made a replica blue ribbon which she sent to Dale. It has pride of place, next to her quilt, displayed proudly on her bedroom wall, together with a picture of Rita's quilt.

Dale is also involved in a block swap with Edel in Germany. Dale is making Fan blocks and Edel is making Basket blocks. Dale makes two of each block and sends one to Edel, who does the same. As the result of a similar block exchange with Rita in America, Dale has many finished quilts.

Rather than being discouraged by the constant workload with deadlines to be met, Dale and Frances continue to be excited by their involvement in international friendship quilts and the people who make them.

At the same time, Dale and Frances worked on a small progressive friendship quilt with Beth and Alma from New Jersey. The small progressive quilt is similar to the large one, but has a starting block of 20 cm (8 in) and only three borders. Each step took about six weeks with completed quilt tops returned to their owners in eight months.

As well as being active members of Eastwood Patchwork Quilters, which involves them in the making of many friendship blocks including the challenge friendship blocks, Dale prepares cut-outs for Christmas for all her quilting pen friends around the world.

Just prior to Christmas 1994, she received a parcel from Rita in the United States. In it were twenty-five small butterfly blocks, ready for assembly. On the parcel was 'Don't Open Before Christmas' but Dale confesses to having the quilt completely finished before Christmas Day!

SHARED SCRAPS, 155 cm x 230 cm, 1995.
Made by Dale Ritson from 530 shared scraps

OVER TO YOU

This section of the book gives instructions for making some wonderful friendship quilts. Each one is an actual friendship quilt, made by friendship groups from all over Australia. You are certain to feel inspired to form a friendship group, after reading about the exciting quilts that others are making.

Forming a friendship group is a very easy process – all you need is a group of willing friends. Remember that the McLaren Vale Quilters, whose wonderful quilts are featured throughout this book, were originally a group of spinners who decided to make each other a quilt. Only a few of their group knew anything about quiltmaking, so your willing friends don't have to be experienced quilters or even quilters at all. All they need is a willingness to learn and someone to teach them.

Try to keep your group to around twelve members. This way everyone gets their blocks quickly enough so they don't lose their enthusiasm. Of course, this is not a hard-and-fast rule.

Once you are all enthused, there are some decisions to be made and guidelines to be established so that your group can run smoothly. First, decide how many you want in your friendship group and whether your group is to remain fixed. It is important to establish this in the beginning and that this number remains constant throughout the project. It can be a problem if late starters join the group, as they won't have made blocks for every member of the group.

Second, determine what restrictions you want on the type of block to be made. Some restrictions could be:

▣ No appliqué.

▣ No more than twenty pieces for a pieced block.

▣ No smaller than 15 cm (6 in).

▣ Only cotton fabrics are to be used.

▣ Blocks must be complex (challenge friendship group).

▣ No embroidery on the block.

You may decide that you are happy to have no restrictions on the blocks and accept any proposed design. Some groups use the more difficult and complex blocks as a learning tool for their less experienced members. Just keep in mind that the blocks are meant to be friendship blocks. You don't want to end up alienating your friends because they have had to spend hours and hours struggling to make your block.

Third, decide what time is to be allowed for the making of each block. Most groups allow one month for completion, while some groups expect the completed block to be handed in sooner. Castle Hill Quilters agreed to complete their blocks in three weeks to allow for every member in their group to have their set of blocks completed during the bicentennial celebrations of 1988. This was a fast and frantic pace that they were able to maintain because they had a fixed goal.

Fourth, decide what each person in your group will receive in their friendship block kit. You must include the pattern and instructions on how best to construct the block. Other inclusions could be:

▣ Prepared templates.

▣ Fabric for the background or for inclusion some-where in the block.

▣ All the fabrics, either cut ready for machine-piecing, or marked for hand-piecing.

▣ Diagram of the quilt to be made from blocks.

▣ Colour preferences and mood preferences, for example pretty pinks, lavenders and lemon for a budding ballerina's bedroom.

At Eastwood Patchwork Quilters, we decided that each kit would contain the templates with a pattern sheet as well, showing block design and instructions on how to make the block. No block had more than thirty pieces and there was no appliqué allowed. If the block only had ten pieces or less, you were allowed to ask for two blocks to be made.

Fifth, to determine who will go first, put everyone's name in a hat, and draw them out in turn, recording the order and the date they are to hand out their instructions. Each member of the group should receive a copy of the draw, so they know when it is their turn. As well as circulating everyone's names, it is often helpful to include addresses and phone numbers for any tardy block makers.

Finally, you might want your friendship group to be an opportunity for instruction from a teacher, so she would choose each block to feature a specific technique. At the end of each time period, the completed blocks could be put in a bag and the lucky winner drawn out.

Whatever rules your group decides on, make sure everyone is happy with the decision and understands them. Now you are ready to begin.

GETTING STARTED

The following instructions are presented in such a way that, once you have chosen the design you like the most, you can simply photocopy the instructions and hand them out to your friends. The instruction include a block diagram, a piecing diagram and full-sized templates. As all the quilts here are friendship quilts, no fabric requirements are included. Most of the fabric for the blocks will come from your friends and you may decide to change the setting of the blocks to suit the number of blocks you receive, or add borders, as you prefer.

Each block can be made by hand or machine. To facilitate this, each template given has two lines. The outer, solid line is the cutting line, and the inner broken line is the sewing line. The lines are 7.5 mm apart (a little over ¼ in). Please use the inner dotted line when preparing templates for hand-piecing and the outer solid line when preparing templates for machine-piecing.

Details of the processes involved in piecing, appliqué and construction of a quilt are not included in this book. It is assumed that someone in your friendship group has this basic knowledge or that you have other resources you can call on. There are, in fact, many fine books available for you to refer to that are entirely devoted to basic quiltmaking. *Creative Traditional Quiltmaking* by Karen Fail (J. B. Fairfax Press, 1995) will provide you with all the information you require.

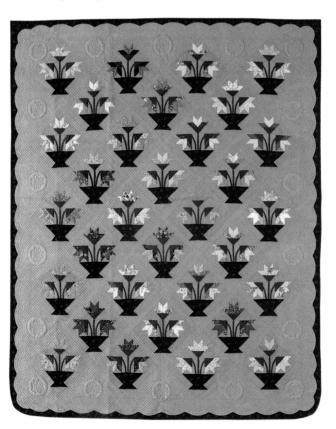

LABOUR OF LOVE, *205 cm x 255 cm, 1994.*
Made by the Eastwood Patchwork Quilters for Leigh Swain

DENISE'S SMOOTHING IRON QUILT

In true friendship quilt tradition, this quilt provides a generous space for messages and loving words.

Block used: Smoothing Iron

Block size: 17 cm (7 in) triangle

Quilt size: 64 blocks are needed for a 130 cm x 194 cm (51 in x 76½ in) quilt

MATERIALS SUPPLIED

Cream homespun for the centre of the block

INSTRUCTIONS

※ Please provide two other fabrics to complete the block. Choose fabrics that have an old-fashioned look.

※ Cut the following pieces:

1 A from cream homespun

3 B from one of your fabrics

3 C from the other fabric

Block Diagram

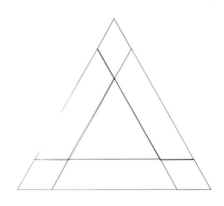

Piecing Diagram

※ Complete the block, following the piecing diagram.

※ Note that the triangle in the centre of the block can be pointing down or up. In your block, place the triangle pointing .... Sign your name on the cream triangle, using a permanent pen, or embroidery or paint, as was done in Victorian times. You may wish to use one of the ornate designs to be seen in various publications. If so, photocopy the design and, while it is still fresh (less than two hours old), iron it into place on the fabric. The final result will be lighter than the photocopy and reversed.

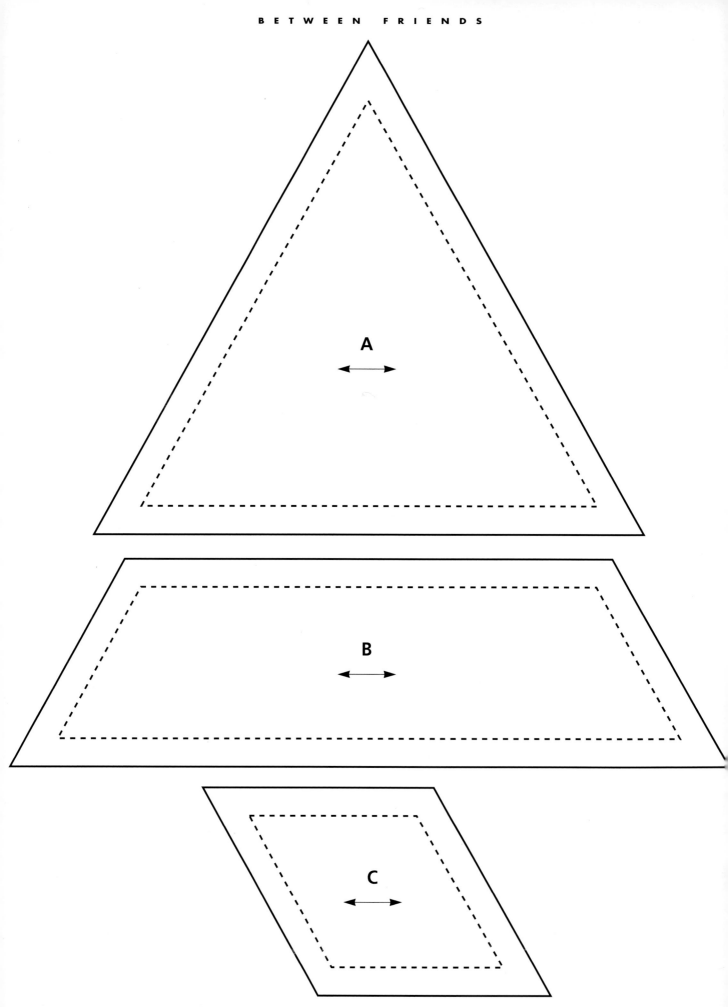

DENISE'S SMOOTHING IRON

For this quilt, I shared fabrics that I had purchased from a Reverse Garbage shop with my friends and ended up with a wonderful mix of zany blocks. My mother, my five sisters and their daughters, as well as my patchwork friends, made blocks for me. At work, I even held lunchtime workshops in piecing and everyone decorated their blocks at home. I treasure my quilt and all the wonderful messages on it.

THESE BLOCKS WERE MADE BY FAMILY, QUILTING FRIENDS AND WORK FRIENDS FROM CASTLE HILL, NEW SOUTH WALES, 1995, FOR DENISE EAST.

FOREVER FRIENDS

Combining the simple Log Cabin blocks with hearts, a lasting symbol of friendship, makes a wonderful quilt to be treasured.

Block used: Log Cabin Heart, adapted from '*A Celebration of Hearts*', by Jean Wells

Block size: 20 cm (8 in)

Quilt size: 64 blocks are needed for a 198 cm x 267 cm (78 in x 105 in) quilt

MATERIALS SUPPLIED

Aqua square background for appliqué

INSTRUCTIONS

▦ Prepare a heart in the colour of your choice and appliqué it to the aqua square, using your preferred method of appliqué. Embroider your name on the heart.

▦ Choose shades of the same colour for the logs, varying the colour from light to dark. Cut 4 cm (1½ in) wide strips from each fabric for the logs. These measurements include a 6 mm (¼ in) seam allowance. You will need four light, four medium and two dark strips of your chosen colour. Attach them to only two sides of the aqua square following the diagram for order of placement. Trim each strip to the required length after it is stitched.

Block Diagram

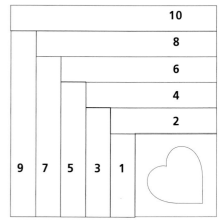

Piecing Diagram

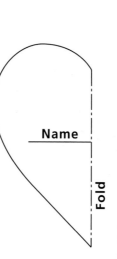

Name

Fold

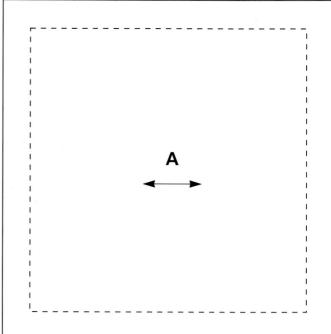

A

FOREVER FRIENDS

While delighting in the heart motif as a symbol of friendship, I was keen to put an 'Aussie' stamp on my quilt. So gum leaves and gumnuts, cockatoos and butterflies feature in the crosshatched aqua borders. As a recently arrived American, I just love my quilt. What a welcome to Tasmania and what an assurance of friendship to a newcomer.

THESE BLOCKS WERE MADE BY THE TASMANIAN QUILTERS GUILD, THE LAUNCESTON PATCHWORKERS AND QUILTERS AND THE TUESDAY QUILTERS, ALL OF TASMANIA, 1990, FOR TINY KENNEDY.

AUTUMN BASKETS

Tiny baskets create a treasure to remember friends by.
Temporarily gluing paper templates to the fabric
makes handling the tiny pieces easier.

Block used: Flower Basket

Block size: 8 cm (3 in)

Quilt size: 9 pieced blocks are needed for a 45 cm (18 in) square quilt

MATERIALS SUPPLIED

White fabric for the background

INSTRUCTIONS

▦ Copy or draft the entire block onto grid paper, using a sharp pencil. Cut out carefully on the lines and paste the paper templates onto the fabric, taking note of the grain lines. Cut out the fabric, leaving seam allowances as you would normally do when you mark fabric. You can prepare plastic templates and mark the fabric if you prefer. If you choose the latter method, make sure you sew along the inside of the pencil line, so that you preserve the size of the block.

▦ Cut the following pieces:

6 A from an autumn-toned fabric (you may make a scrappy basket or use only one fabric)

2 B from a different autumn-toned fabric

8 A, 2 C and 1 D from the white fabric

▦ Using the paper templates as a guide and following the piecing diagram, hand-piece the block.

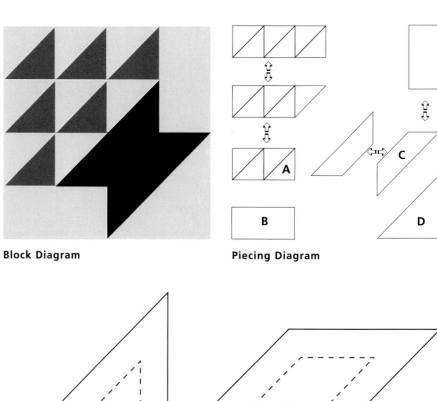

Block Diagram

Piecing Diagram

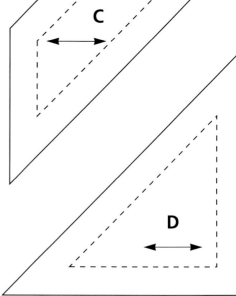

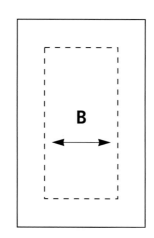

58

AUTUMN BASKETS

Our group had only just started, and we wanted to make friendship quilts that we would be sure to finish, so we decided to make miniatures. Often the templates were so small that marking the fabric increased the size of the block. So we resorted to using paper templates. I was delighted with my tiny baskets and pleased I had chosen a spotted fabric for the alternating blocks. That meant I could simply follow the dots to complete the crosshatching. Long after the quilt was finished, I took it off the wall and quilted the white inner border, a finishing touch I had not thought necessary when my little quilt was first deemed 'finished'.

THESE BLOCKS WERE MADE BY GOOD INTENT QUILTERS,
RYDE, NEW SOUTH WALES, 1989, FOR LOIS COOK.

FRIENDLY FANS

Create fanciful bow ties with the traditional
Grandmother's Fan block set in this unusual way.

Block used: Grandmother's Fan

Block size: 20 cm (8 in)

**Quilt size: 49 blocks are needed for a
160 cm x 190 cm (63 in x 75 in) quilt**

MATERIALS SUPPLIED

Square of cream homespun with a
20 cm (8 in) square marked on it
Blue fabric for the fan centre

INSTRUCTIONS

▦ Prepare templates A and B,
following the general instructions
on page 52.

▦ Using template A, cut 6 from 6
different blue print fabrics – a little
pink or mauve is quite acceptable.

▦ Cut 1 B from the blue fabric
supplied.

Block Diagram

▦ Join the fan sections together.
For a smooth curve, run a small
running stitch, just inside the seam
allowance of each curved segment.
Place the template on the stitching
line on the wrong side of each fabric
section and draw up the thread.
Press the segment firmly, giving a
nice smooth curved edge.

▦ Appliqué the fan into position
with the edges matching the background edges.

▦ Embroider your initials on the
completed block.

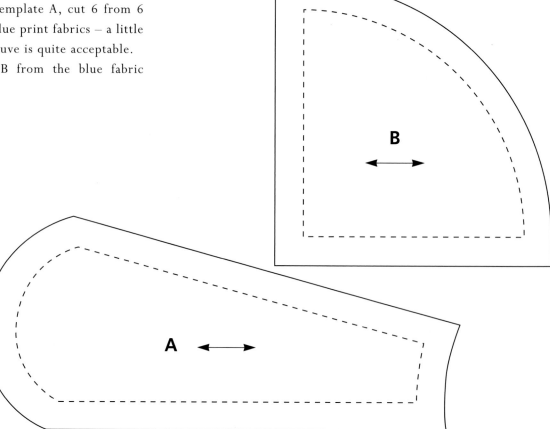

FRIENDLY FANS

Soft dusky pinks and blues are my very favourite colours, and I really like traditional patterns. When I saw a photograph of a quilt with the Grandmother's Fan block set in such a pretty way, I decided to make this my next friendship block. Everyone embroidered their initials on their block, so I can read them and remember who helped me make my delightful quilt.

THESE BLOCKS WERE MADE BY THE EPPING QUILTERS, NEW SOUTH WALES, 1995, FOR ELAINE GALLEN.

CHATELAINE FRIENDSHIP

The charm of this quilt is in its simplicity. A simple sixteen-patch block divided diagonally into light and dark creates a visual delight.

Block used: Shaded Four-patch

Block size: 30 cm (12 in)

Quilt size: 16 blocks are needed for a 180 cm (71 in) square quilt

MATERIALS SUPPLIED

Some floral fabrics to set the mood

INSTRUCTIONS

▦ Please supplement the fabrics provided with florals from your own collection. Keep dark fabrics on one side of the block and light fabrics on the other. Remember that the dark fabrics only need to be darker than the light fabrics in the block.

▦ Cut the following pieces:

6 A from the light fabrics

6 A from the dark fabrics

4 B from the light fabrics

4 B from the dark fabrics

▦ When piecing the block, join the light and dark triangles first to form four squares, then complete the block, following the piecing diagram.

▦ Embroider your initials on your block, when it is finished.

Block Diagram

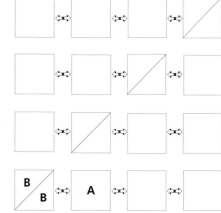

Piecing Diagram

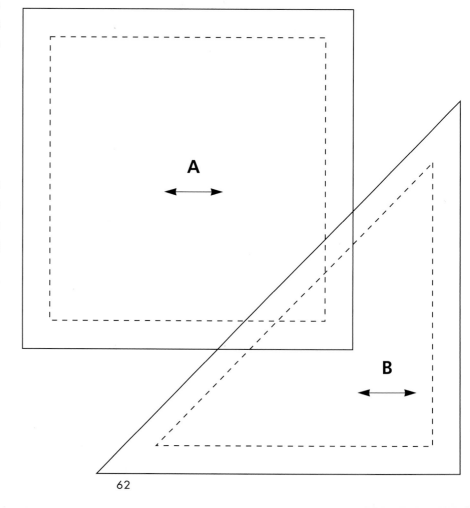

CHATELAINE FRIENDSHIP

When these blocks were made in 1989, nobody had heard of colour-wash, and the variety of florals was limited. I was keen to keep my friendship block simple, while creating a dynamic quilt. I achieved this by extending the pieced blocks into the border and accentuated the catherine wheel effect by quilting with straight lines.

THESE BLOCKS WERE MADE BY THE CHATELAINE QUILTERS, SYDNEY, NEW SOUTH WALES, 1989 FOR CAROLYN SULLIVAN.

DAISIES

With such a variety of fabrics used in the petals, and each alternate block cut from a different fabric, this quilt achieves a wonderful scrappy thirties look.

Block used: Daisy

Block size: 20 cm (8 in)

Quilt size: 48 daisy blocks and 35 plain blocks are needed for a 170 cm x 225 cm (67 in x 88 in) quilt

MATERIALS SUPPLIED

22 cm (9 in) cream square for the background

INSTRUCTIONS

▨ The finished quilt should look like a scrappy, old quilt with each petal in a different fabric.

▨ Trace the templates onto template plastic. A coin with a 3 cm (1¼ in) diameter is a useful template for the centre circle.

▨ Mark 1 petal on the right side of each of 8 different fabrics.

Block Diagram

▨ Fold the background square in half horizontally and vertically and along each diagonal to locate the centre and provide guidelines for placement of the petals. Press the folds.

▨ Baste under the seam allowance on each petal. Put a pin through the tips of the petals, then through the

centre of the background, then stick the pin through into the ironing board cover to anchor it. Carefully spread out the petals and line them up on the pressed lines on the background fabric. Pin each petal into place as you go. Each petal slightly overlaps the preceding one. At the end, tuck the edge of the last petal under the first one.

▨ Centre the coin on the petals and lightly mark its outline with a pencil. Trim each petal to within 6 mm (¼ in) of the pencil line to reduce bulk.

▨ Appliqué the petals, using a thread to match each petal.

▨ Using a solid fabric of your choice and the round template, mark the circle on the right side of the fabric. Appliqué the circle in the centre of the petals.

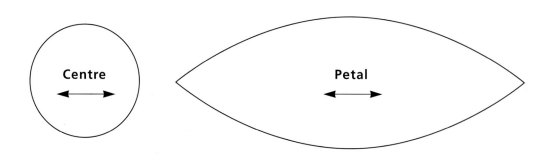

Centre

Petal

DAISIES

Having made many friendship quilts, my group decided that it was time to make blocks with a challenge. So I chose this overlapping appliqué flower. I belong to several groups who all wanted to join in, so I have blocks from my friends in all my groups. Some of the blocks were cut out by three quilting friends in the United States and I pieced them. It was a great way to get an interesting variety in the fabrics used.

THESE BLOCKS WERE MADE BY THE EASTWOOD PATCHWORK QUILTERS, THE GOOD INTENT QUILTERS AND THE HILLSIDE QUILTERS, ALL OF NEW SOUTH WALES, 1991, FOR LEIGH SWAIN. (SOME BLOCKS WERE CUT-AROUND BLOCKS WHICH LEIGH STITCHED TOGETHER). THIS QUILT WAS INSPIRED BY 'LENA' QUILT ART ENGAGEMENT CALENDAR 1990.

BEARLY THERE FRIENDSHIP QUILT

Using a traditional block and the same fabric for the sashing strips, the setting triangles and the borders allow the blocks in this delightful quilt to float on a sea of green.

Block used: Farmer's Daughter

Block size: 25 cm (10 in)

Quilt size: 23 blocks are needed for a 156 cm x 241 cm (61 in x 95 in) quilt

MATERIALS SUPPLIED

Cream homespun for the background

INSTRUCTIONS

▨ You will need two, three or four scraps of various pink and green fabrics.

▨ Prepare templates A, B and C. (See page 52 for how to prepare templates.)

▨ Cut the following pieces:

4 A and 4 B from the cream home-spun

4 C and 4 C(r) from one of the pink and green fabrics or 4 C from one fabric and 4 C(r) from another fabric

1 A for the centre square

4 A for the surrounding squares from a different pink or green fabric

▨ Assemble the block following the piecing diagram.

Block Diagram

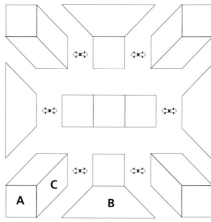

Piecing Diagram

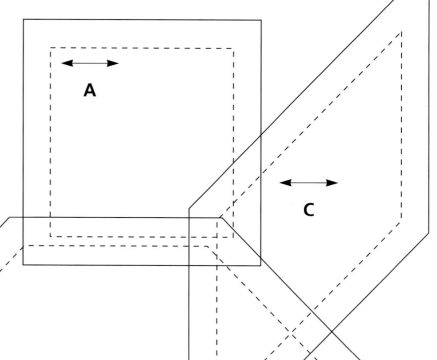

BEARLY THERE FRIENDSHIP QUILT

To herald our adventures into friendship blocks, the group chose this design and the colour scheme. We seemed very casual about the whole process and I wasn't particularly keen to win the finished blocks as I had planned a Bear's Paw block for my quilt. Having recovered from the shock of winning, by the time I had put the quilt together completely by hand and finished the hand-quilted grid, I really loved it. I find myself thinking as I look at each block, 'Ah yes! That's so like Sue or Judy'. It's wonderful to have such a permanent reminder of each of my quilting friends.

THESE BLOCKS WERE MADE BY THE BEARLY THERE QUILTERS, HORNSBY, NEW SOUTH WALES, 1993, FOR JENNY EVANS.

MY LITTLE GIRLS

Sunbonnet Sue again captures everyone's heart as she chases butterflies and catches balloons in this traditional block.

Block used: Sunbonnet Sue

Block size: 30 cm (12 in)

Quilt size: 15 blocks are needed for this 110 cm x 180 cm (43 in x 71 in) quilt

MATERIALS SUPPLIED

35 cm (14 in) white square
Double-sided fusible webbing

INSTRUCTIONS

▨ Choose any colours you like, except green!

▨ Trace the pattern pieces onto the paper side of the fusible webbing. Do not remove the paper at this stage. Note, when extra is needed for the underlap it is denoted by the dotted lines. Cut out each pattern piece leaving 1 cm ($^3/_8$ in) outside the pencil line. Iron these pieces onto the wrong side of your selected fabric, using a dry iron on the wool setting. Turn the fabric over and firmly press on the webbed area. Cut out each piece on the pencil lines. Peel off the paper backing.

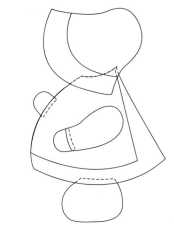

Block Diagram

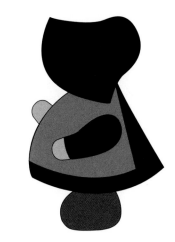

Piecing Diagram

▨ Assemble the motif on the background fabric, making sure that your Sunbonnet Sue is in the centre of the square. Be sure to place the underlaps correctly. Use the numbers on the templates to guide you. Your Sunbonnet Sue is now facing right. Press the pieces lightly into place, one at a time. When you are happy with the assembly, put a light pressing cloth over the lot and press again, very firmly. Turn over and press again on the wrong side.

▨ Hand-stitch in herringbone or buttonhole stitch around the edges of all the pieces. Add embellishments such as flowers, insects and the like, then embroider your name in the bottom left corner in a colour to match your Sunbonnet Sue.

MY LITTLE GIRLS

I had just discovered appliqué in 1990 and fell in love with Sunbonnet Sue. A friendship quilt was a great way to get the blocks quickly, as I was not convinced that I would finish the fifteen blocks needed. Each block was quilted before assembly, with a sun in one corner, clouds in another and the outline of hills, grass and a crazy path along the bottom. The quilted blocks were then joined using the 'quilt as you go' method. Lastly the broderie anglaise frill was added. I was delighted!

THESE BLOCKS WERE MADE BY THE MARION QUILTERS, SOUTH AUSTRALIA, 1992, FOR MOYA MARSHALL.

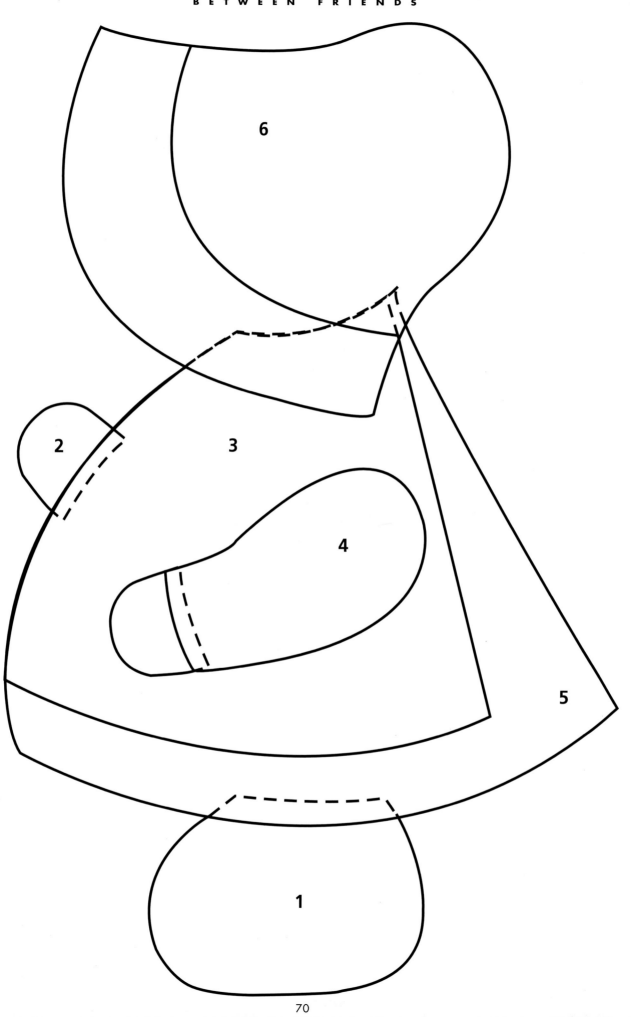

SCOTTIES

Scottie dogs with smart plaid jackets line up ready to march straight into your heart. A dog biscuit provides the template for the unique quilting pattern.

Block used: Scottie

Block size: 25 cm (10 in)

Quilt size: 15 blocks are needed for a 135 cm x 205 cm (53 in x 81 in) quilt

MATERIALS SUPPLIED

Cream fabric for the background
Black fabric for the body

INSTRUCTIONS

▨ Use a plaid or checked fabric for the Scottie's coat.

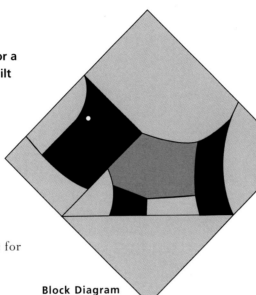

Block Diagram

▨ With your finished block, include enough of your plaid or checked fabric for four 9.5 cm (3¾ in) squares.

▨ Cut the following pieces:
  1 E, 1 F, 1 G, 1 H, 1 I, 1 J and 1 K from the background fabric
    1 A, 1 B, 1 C from the black fabric
  1 D from the plaid or checked fabric

▨ Piece the block, following the piecing diagram.

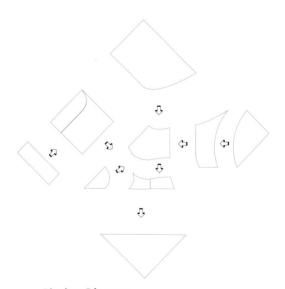

Piecing Diagram

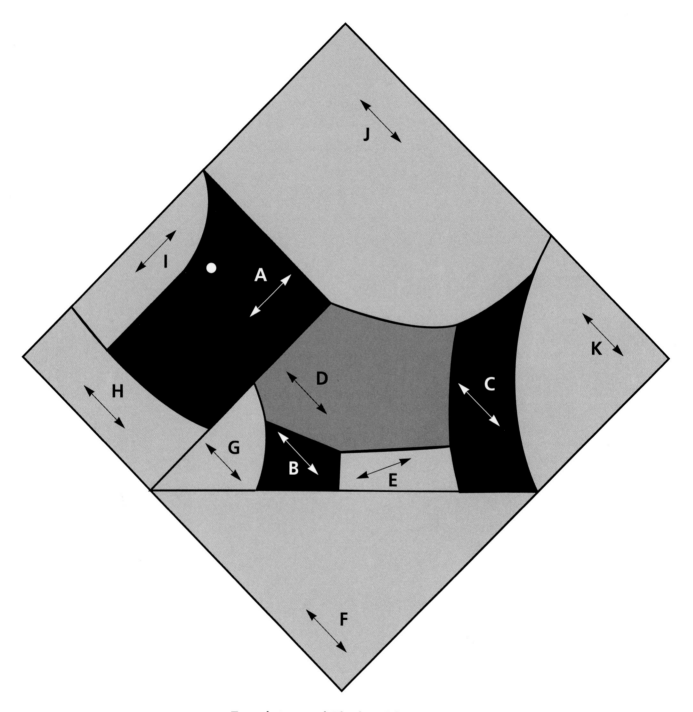

Templates and Piecing Diagram

Note: Templates are given at 50% of actual size. Enlarge to 100%

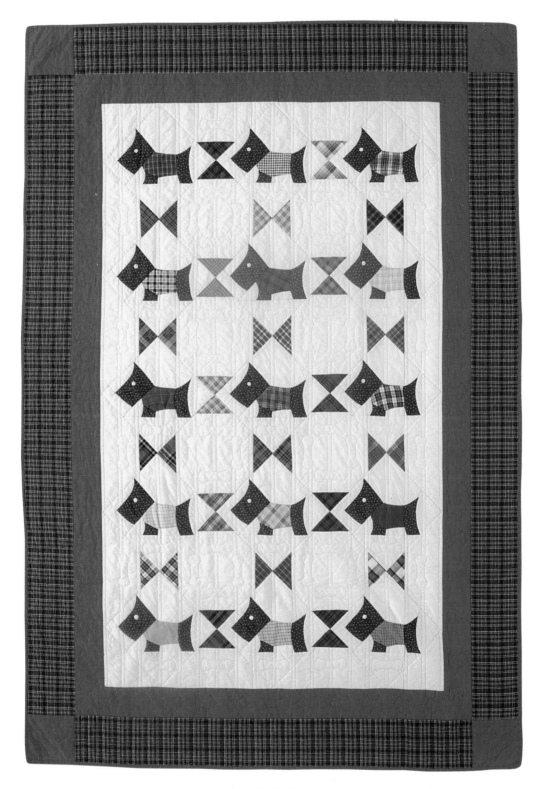

SCOTTIES

I thought this quilt would be a lot of fun to make and would be enjoyed by my family. My friends chose plaids that reflected their preferences in fabrics, so I can tell who made which block. One of the Eastwood quilters, Lea Lane, suggested using the Snowball block in the alternate rows, an idea which worked well. For the quilting, I traced around a dog biscuit to make the template. Finally, I quilted miniature Scotties in the red border.

THESE BLOCKS WERE MADE BY EASTWOOD PATCHWORK QUILTERS,
NEW SOUTH WALES, 1991, FOR EVELYN FINNAN.

BUTTERFLY REQUIEM

This pretty version of the traditional Dresden Plate block creates a quilt with an old-world charm that looks like it was made many years ago.

Block used: Modified Dresden Plate

Block size: 30 cm (12 in)

Quilt size: 25 blocks are needed for a 185 cm (73 in) square quilt

MATERIALS SUPPLIED

32 cm (12½ in) square of cream homespun

Cream homespun for the centre circle

One of my favourite fabrics to use, if you want to

INSTRUCTIONS

✦ Prepare templates for the petal (A) and the leaf (B).

✦ Cut the following pieces:

16 A from scraps, but every petal does not have to be different

16 B from colours that coordinate with the petals, but the leaves do not have to be green

1 B from the homespun

1 B from thin cardboard

Block Diagram

✦ Sew two of the petals together and place a leaf diamond between them. Repeat this eight times, then join the pairs to form a circle.

✦ Baste the homespun circle around the cardboard template C. Press. Place the circle in the centre of the ring of petals and appliqué it in place. Remove the basting and take the cardboard out from the back, through the centre hole.

✦ Appliqué the completed plate to the background block, making sure it is centred.

✦ Please embroider your name in the centre circle and appliqué or embroider a butterfly there as well.

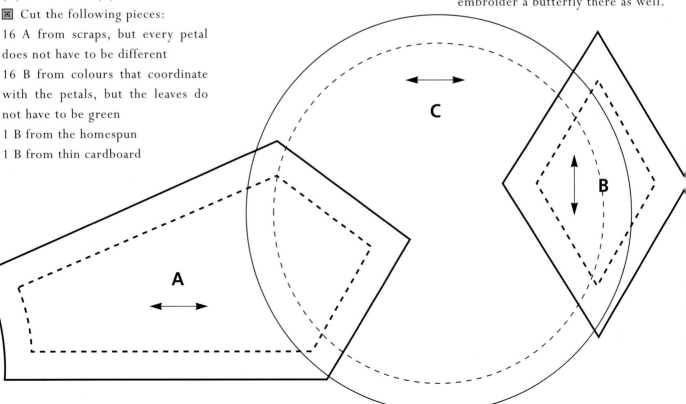

BUTTERFLY REQUIEM

The things that give me pleasure are Botticelli paintings, potpourri, old roses, and the colours of the sea at dusk, so my friendship quilt needed to look as though it had been made in a bygone time, faded by years of loving wear and care. I chose greyed shades of green, pink and blue, with lots of lovely scrappy fabrics from my friends. They added butterflies to their completed blocks, and I quilted butterflies on the ivy leaf quilting design. The butterflies are symbolic of the spirits of my three friends, who died while the quilt was being made, but who are now flying free.

THESE BLOCKS WERE MADE BY QUILT CONNECTIONS, WESTERN AUSTRALIA, 1990, FOR CYNTHIA BAKER.

ROSE STAR

The colours of a bygone era are used in this quilt to give it an old-world look, as the rose stars float on a background of cream, their black points providing sharp contrast to the otherwise gentle colours.

Block used: Rose Star (an Alice Brooks pattern)

Block size: 48 cm (19 in) diameter hexagon

Quilt size: 22 complete blocks and 6 half blocks are needed for a 2.5 m (2³⁄₄ yd) square quilt

MATERIALS SUPPLIED
Cream fabric for the background

INSTRUCTIONS
▣ Only one kite-shaped template is required for this block.

▣ Please choose fabric with an old-world look.

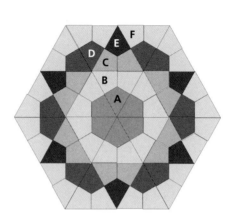

Block Diagram

▣ Make the points on the rose out of a black fabric with a small print.

▣ For each block, cut the following pieces, using the template provided:

6 from a light fabric for A

12 from a dark fabric for B

12 from a medium fabric for C

12 from a medium dark fabric for D

6 from the black fabric with a small print for E

24 from the cream fabric, supplied, for F

▣ Piece the block, following the block diagram.

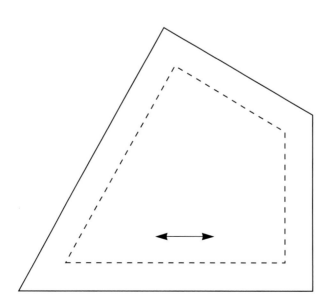

ROSE STAR

As the block, Rose Star, used only one template I thought it would provide a challenge for the group. They loved the look of the finished quilt and it now covers my mother's old eiderdown, remade to fit the quilt.

THESE BLOCKS WERE MADE BY THE GOOD INTENT QUILTERS, EPPING, NEW SOUTH WALES, 1994, FOR ELIZABETH BOSWELL.

TIME FOR TEA

Piecing in strips and a controlled palette make
this quilt a real winner and a delightful reminder
of shared moments over a cup of tea.

Blocks used: Teapot, Cup and Saucer

Block size: 30 cm (12 in)

**Quilt size: 16 blocks are needed for a
168 cm (66 in) square quilt**

MATERIALS SUPPLIED

Cup and saucer print fabric

Pale blue print fabric

Medium blue fabric

White fabric for the background

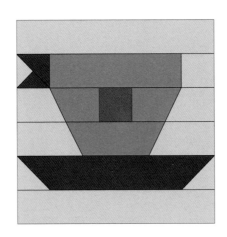

Block Diagram

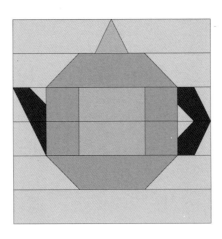

Block Diagram

INSTRUCTIONS

▦ Decide if you want to make a teapot or a cup and saucer. Following the appropriate piecing diagram, prepare a 30 cm (12 in) square. Divide it into 5 cm (2 in) squares. Draft your chosen design and prepare your templates.

▦ The blocks are easily pieced into five horizontal strips which are then joined together.

▦ You may add touches of one other fabric of your choice.

▦ If you wish, you may appliqué a curved handle on the cup, rather than piece it.

TIME FOR TEA

Inspired by a painting of teapots and cups, I decided to design two blocks for my friends in Burnie to make. Somehow I thought that these blocks really summed up the group well — twelve ladies all gathered round, with cups in hand, sharing tips as they work towards completing their first quilt.

THESE BLOCKS WERE MADE BY THE BURNIE QUILTERS, TASMANIA, 1995, FOR LINDA CARTER.

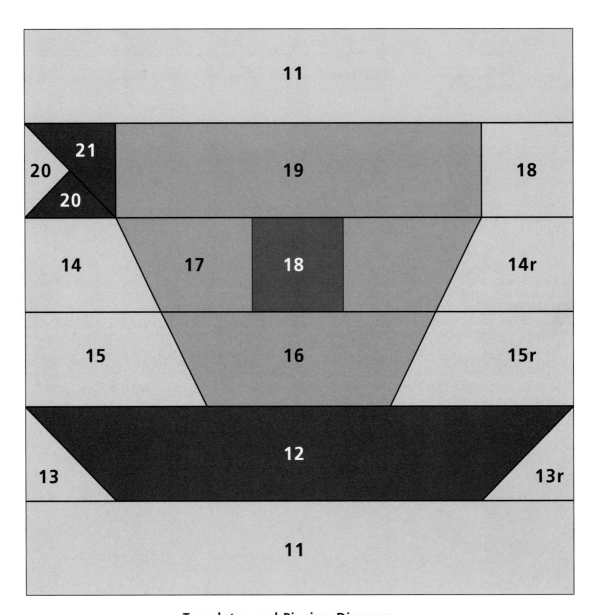

Templates and Piecing Diagram

Note: Templates are given at 50%
of actual size. Enlarge to 100%

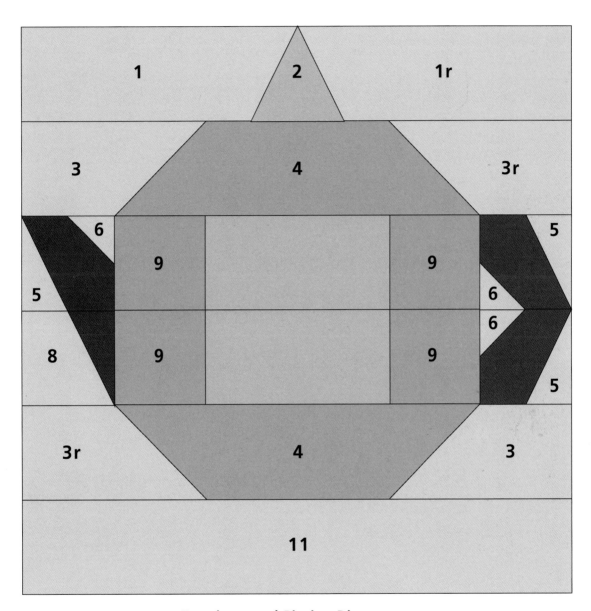

Templates and Piecing Diagram

Note: Templates are given at 50% of actual size. Enlarge to 100%

FAR EAST, FAR OUT, FAR OFF

Original blocks can create fun friendship quilts, especially
when an outlandish batik fabric is the starting point.
A wild border adds the finishing touch.

Block used: original design 'Larraine's Star'

Block size: variable from 7 cm (2¾ in) to 45 cm (17¾ in)

Quilt size: the number of blocks needed varies, depending on the sizes chosen. This quilt is 140 cm x 180 cm (55 in x 71 in).

MATERIALS SUPPLIED

Piece of multicoloured batik

INSTRUCTIONS

※ You only need to use one fabric, other than the one supplied, to complete the block. An unusual or bizarre fabric would be great!

※ The block can be any size, except 30 cm (12 in). No templates are provided. One quarter of a 24 cm (9½ in) block is given as a guide.

Block Diagram

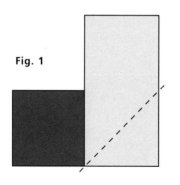

Fig. 1

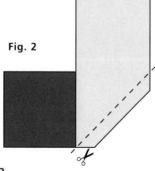

Fig. 2

Fig. 3

Decide what size you want your block to be and draft the appropriate templates. Note that only one-quarter of the block needs to be drafted.

※ Quick machine- and hand-piecing construction tip: a block can be made from four long and four short rectangles, cut from each of the two fabrics. Add your preferred seam allowance to the finished sizes as calculated below:

Finished length of long rectangle A = finished size of block divided by 2

Finished length of short rectangle B = finished size of block divided by three

Finished width of both rectangles = finished size of block divided by six

※ Piece the block, following figures 1-3 and the block diagram.

FAR EAST, FAR OUT, FAR OFF

Our group has attempted many difficult blocks as we endeavour to challenge ourselves and improve our skills. I decided to set an easy task to show that patchwork does not have to have a lot of pieces to be interesting. The only 45 cm (17¾ in) block was pieced, using a dinosaur print with fluorescent orange glasses. It dominated the layout — no matter where it was placed. In the end, I split it into several parts. My asymmetrical layout meant I had gaps to fill. For these, I used special fabrics collected from friends over the years. Even the backing fabric, a bright blue and red print, was donated by a friend who confessed to not sleeping at night while it was in her home.

THESE BLOCKS WERE MADE BY THE RUSTY PINS QUILTERS, GLENBROOK, NEW SOUTH WALES, 1994, FOR LARRAINE SCOULER.

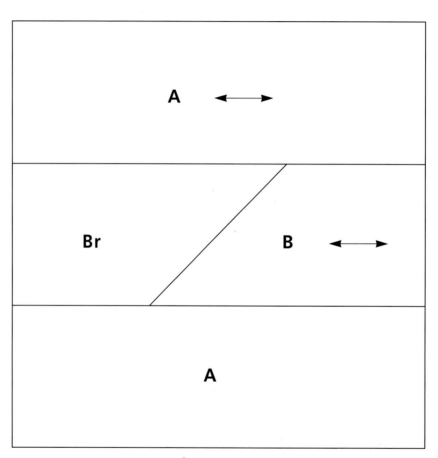

1/4 Block

AMISH SPARKLE

Using the traditional Amish colours against a black
background in a mosaic tile pattern creates a stunning
graphic effect in this quilt.

The mosaic tile pattern is adapted from *Mosaic Tile Designs* by Susan Johnson (Dover Publications. New York)

Block used: Mosaic Tile

Block size: 30 cm (12 in)

Quilt size: 24 blocks are needed for a 162 cm x 220 cm (64 in x 87 in) quilt

MATERIALS SUPPLIED

Black fabric for the background

INSTRUCTIONS

▣ The quilt is to be in Amish colours, from the cool side of the colour wheel, that is dark red through to green. Only plain fabrics are to be used to maintain the Amish theme. You will need to select fabric in three colours.

Block Diagram

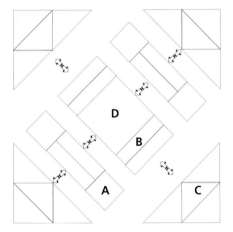

Piecing Diagram

▣ Prepare templates A, B, C and D. (See page 52 for how to prepare your own templates.)

▣ Cut the following pieces:

4 A from fabric one

4 B from fabric two

4 B from fabric three

4 C from fabric three

12 C from the black fabric

4 C from fabric two

1 D from the black fabric

▣ Assemble the block, following the piecing diagram.

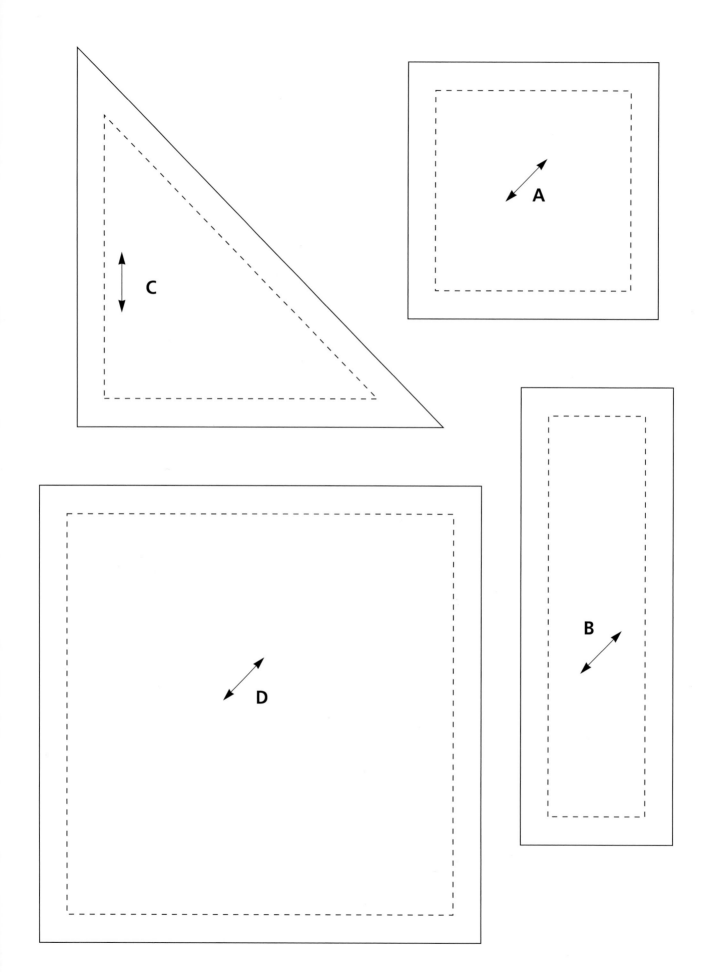

AMISH SPARKLE

My block with twenty-eight pieces just fell within the limit of thirty pieces for a friendship block, set by my group. I really love the Amish designs and thought this tile pattern, although not traditionally Amish, would work well using an Amish palette. I couldn't have been more pleased with my blocks and find them a lasting memory of friends in my quilting group at that time.

THESE BLOCKS WERE MADE BY EASTWOOD PATCHWORK QUILTERS, NEW SOUTH WALES, 1993, FOR JULIE WOODS.

JUDY IN ARABIA

Create a twinkling sea of stars with this simple block. A soft palette adds to the appeal of this quilt. Construction of the top is easy too, with blocks sewn directly together.

Block used: Judy in Arabia

Block size: 21 cm (9 in)

Quilt size: 48 blocks are needed for a 165 cm x 215 cm (65 in x 86 in) quilt

MATERIALS SUPPLIED

No special fabrics needed. Please use your own scraps.

INSTRUCTIONS

▨ You will need four or five fabrics, mostly the aqua and mauve palette and including at least two light, two medium and one dark fabric.

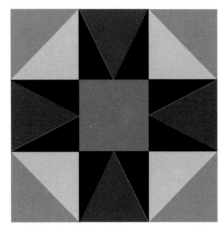

Block Diagram

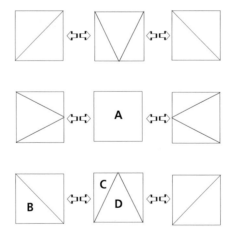

Piecing Diagram

▨ Prepare templates A, B and C. Cut the following pieces:

1 A

4 B from a light fabric for the corners

4 B from a medium or dark fabric to complete the corner squares

8 C for the star points (make sure they provide a good contrast with the corners)

4 D from medium to dark fabrics for between the star points

▨ Assemble the block, following the piecing diagram.

JUDY IN ARABIA

Aqua is my favourite colour. I have decorated my house with an aqua and apricot theme, and especially love the soft aqua walls in my bedroom and my window seat covered in aqua velvet. When I found sample bags of off-cuts of Liberty fabric at the local school fete, I bought the lot — including a wonderful collection of aqua pieces which I decided to include in my friendship quilt. The irregular pieces provided quite a challenge in cutting out, but eventually I had enough blocks prepared to give two to each of my friends at Northbridge Quilters. I still needed to make several blocks myself to complete my wonderful quilt, which has provided the finishing touch to my bedroom.

THESE BLOCKS WERE MADE BY THE NORTHBRIDGE QUILTERS,
NEW SOUTH WALES, 1990, FOR SUSAN KELLY.

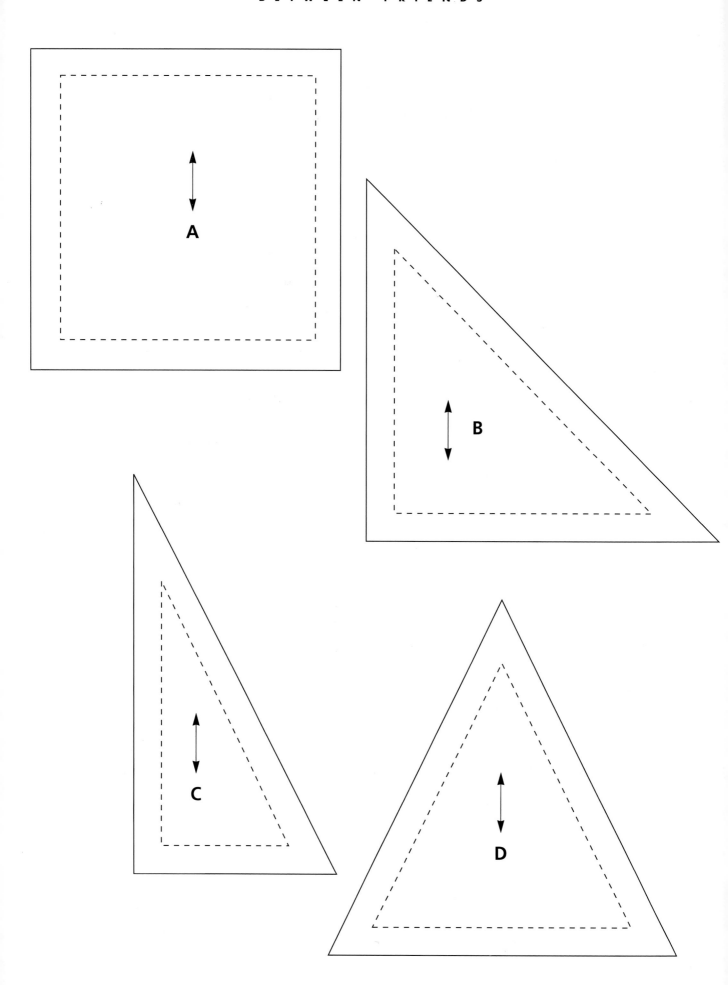

A

B

C

D

MY FRIENDSHIP QUILT

This quilt is made from one version of the Friendship or Album block. The Friendship block retains the characteristic common to all these blocks – the white space in the centre for friends to sign.

Block used: Friendship or Album

Block size: 25 cm (10 in)

Quilt size: 30 blocks are needed for a 150 cm x 180 cm (59 in x 71 in) quilt

MATERIALS SUPPLIED

White fabric for the centre square
Dark fabric for the outer rectangles

INSTRUCTIONS

❖ Use any fabrics that coordinate with the dark fabric that is supplied. The triangles can be calico or cream print fabrics.

Block Diagram

❖ When you are marking the fabric, take care to follow the grain.

❖ Cut the following pieces:
1 A from the white fabric provided
4 B from the dark fabric provided
4 C from a light fabric provided
4 D from a medium value fabric
12 E from a cream fabric
4 F from a cream fabric.

❖ Feel free to embroider a motif, as well as your name, in the white central square.

❖ Assemble the block, following the piecing diagram.

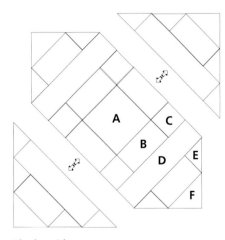

Piecing Diagram

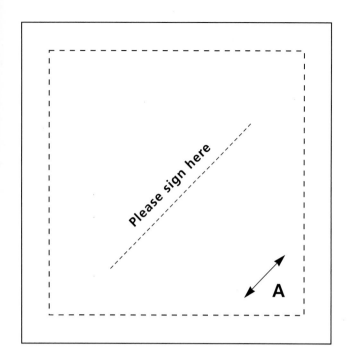

Please sign here

A

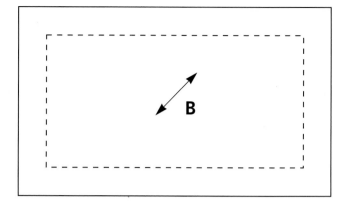

B

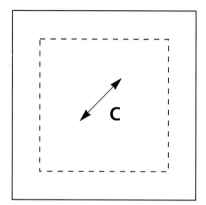

C

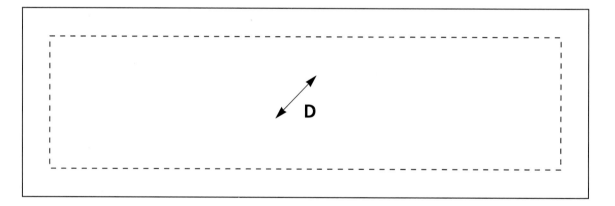

D

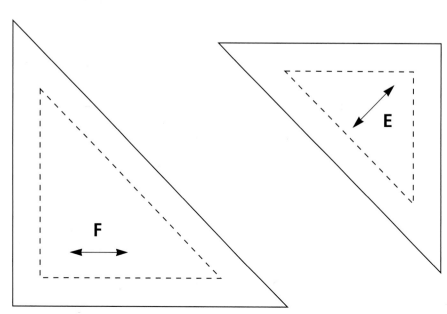

E

F

MY FRIENDSHIP QUILT

Because I really wanted to re-create the look of the old friendship quilts, I was keen to employ one of the patterns traditionally used to record names and messages by friends and family. When the blocks were finished, complete with names and other interesting motifs, I counted ninety-three different fabrics!

THESE BLOCKS WERE MADE BY FRIENDS IN LAUNCESTON, TASMANIA, 1993, FOR LILLIAN ATKINSON.

CHARMING STARS

Every star is different in this delightful scrap quilt, each reflecting
the personality of the maker. The stars are signed, using pen or
thread, with an occasional signature done by machine.

Block used: Five-pointed Star

**Block size: small blocks, 16 cm x
28 cm (6½ in x 11 in), large blocks,
22 cm x 28 cm (8⅝ in x 11 in)**

**Quilt size: 49 blocks are needed for a
172 cm x 220 cm (68 in x 87 in) quilt**

MATERIALS SUPPLIED

Select all the fabrics from your own
collection.

Block Diagram

Block Diagram

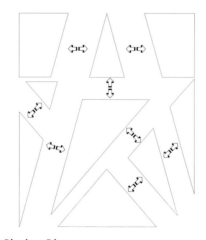

Piecing Diagram

INSTRUCTIONS

▦ You may choose to make a small
or a large star block.

▦ Use the templates provided or
draw up your own full-sized block if
you wish.

▦ When marking the back of the
fabric, make sure you reverse the
irregular-shaped templates A, C, D,
E, G, I, L, K, M, O.

▦ Use fabrics from your own
collection, so the block reflects
your particular style of quiltmaking.

▦ Assemble the block, following
the piecing diagram.

▦ Sign your block.

CHARMING STARS

During my presidency, the tenth anniversary Quilt Show of the Quilters' Guild was held in Sydney in 1992. It was called 'The Decade of Stars' and featured not only members' work, but a retrospective of ten years of Quilt Show favourites. The theme category that year was 'Stars'. The following year's Quilt Show was 'The Charm of Quilts' with the theme category being 'Charm and Scrap Quilts'. Both of these themes are in my friendship quilt, a wonderful reminder of the people I worked with during that time. 'Moving right along' was apparently a favourite saying of mine during committee meetings, but I don't ever remember saying it!

THESE BLOCKS WERE MADE BY THE COMMITTEE AND FRIENDS OF THE QUILTERS' GUILD OF AUSTRALIA FOR KAREN FAIL ON HER RETIREMENT AS PRESIDENT OF THE GUILD 1992-93.

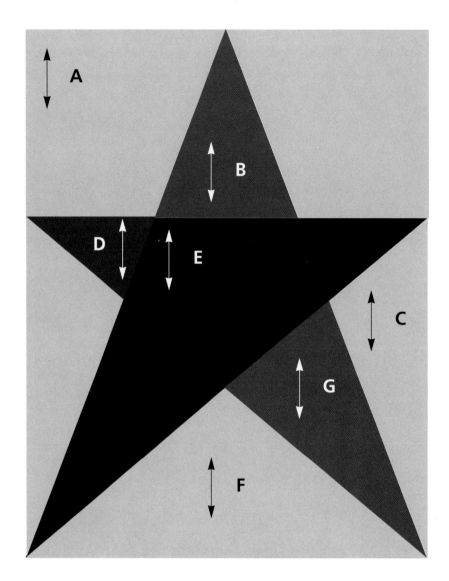

Templates and Piecing Diagram

Note: Templates are given at 50%
of actual size. Enlarge to 100%

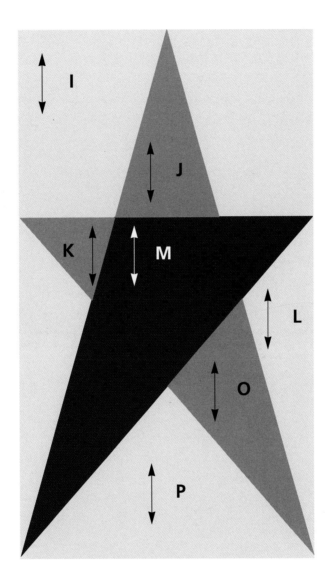

Templates and Piecing Diagram

Note: Templates are given at 50% of actual size. Enlarge to 100%

BOLD AND BEAUTIFUL

A light, bright small quilt, using the same central fabric in each block. No fabrics with white or cream backgrounds are used.

Blocks used: Sawtooth Star and Puss in the Corner

Block size: 16 cm (6 in) (These block sizes are not simple conversions of one another. For ease of drafting, choose to work in either imperial or metric and choose the appropriate block size for your choice. Metric templates are provided.)

Quilt size: 13 Sawtooth Star and 12 Puss in the Corner blocks are needed for a 100 cm (37½ in) square quilt

MATERIALS SUPPLIED

Multicoloured fabric for two centre squares

Templates A, B, C, D, and E

INSTRUCTIONS

▦ Make one Sawtooth Star and one Puss in the Corner block.

▦ For the Sawtooth Star block, cut the following:

1 A from the fabric provided

4 B from a medium value fabric

4 E from a medium value fabric

8 D from a dark fabric.

▦ For the Puss in the Corner block, cut the following:

1 A from the fabric provided

4 B from a dark fabric

4 C from a fabric of your choice

Block Diagram - Sawtooth Star

Block Diagram - Puss in the Corner

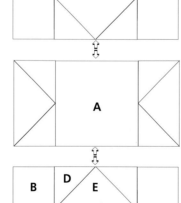

Piecing Diagram

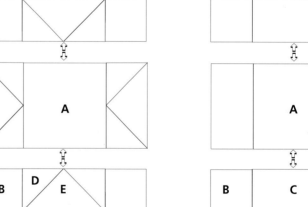

Piecing Diagram

▦ No white or cream background fabrics are to be used.

▦ Use medium and large print fabrics with abandon.

▦ Strong plains work well also.

▦ Assemble the blocks, following the piecing diagram.

BOLD AND BEAUTIFUL

I struggle to use blue in my quiltmaking, so I thought I could get my friends to help. The fabric I chose for the centre square had quite a lot of blue in it (according to me), but my friends saw mainly the many warm hues. In a last-ditch attempt to have a blue quilt, I had to add the cornflower blue border myself!]

THESE BLOCKS WERE MADE BY EASTWOOD PATCHWORK
QUILTERS, NEW SOUTH WALES, 1992, FOR KAREN FAIL.

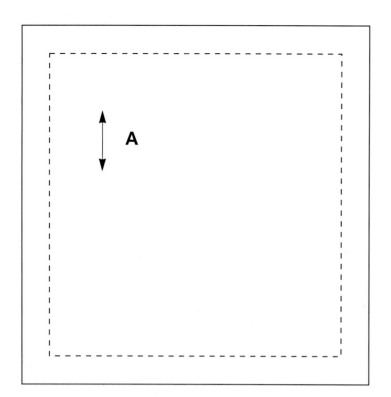

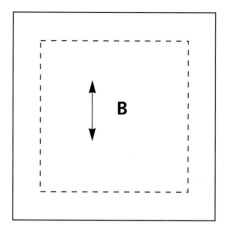

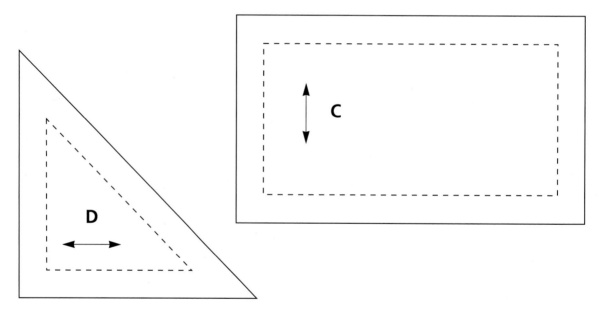

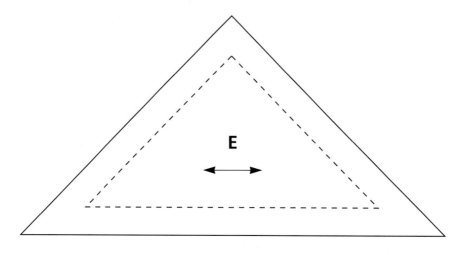

JEWEL OF THE ORIENT

Two simple blocks and a striking colour scheme create a stunning quilt that glows like a Persian carpet.

Block used: Original design, adapted from 'New England Sojourn' *Quiltmaker* **Spring/Summer 1985**

Block size: 24 cm (9 in)

Quilt size: 31 Block 1, 20 red Block 2 and 12 blue Block 2 are needed for a 183 cm x 230 cm (72 in x 90½ in) quilt.

MATERIALS SUPPLIED

Four fabrics are provided so that the quilt will resemble an oriental carpet: turquoise fabric, red or blue fabric, a small khaki print and a large khaki print

INSTRUCTIONS

▩ Please make one Block 1 and two Block 2.

▩ For Block 1, cut the following pieces:

1 C from the turquoise fabric

4 D from the red or blue fabric

4 E from the the large khaki print

▩ For Block 2, cut the following pieces:

4 A from the red or blue fabric

4 B from the small khaki print fabric

▩ Each of the blocks requires simple hand-piecing. Refer to the piecing diagrams.

▩ Use a grey thread to blend in with all the colours.

Block Diagram

Block Diagram

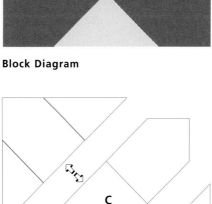

Piecing Diagram

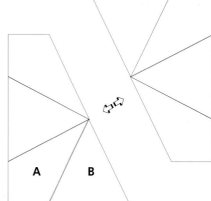

Piecing Diagram

▩ When pressing for Block 2, make sure all the seams face the same way. For Block 1, press the seams in alternate directions to avoid bulk at the joins.

▩ Embroider your name or add a little 'something' especially from you in the turquoise centre.

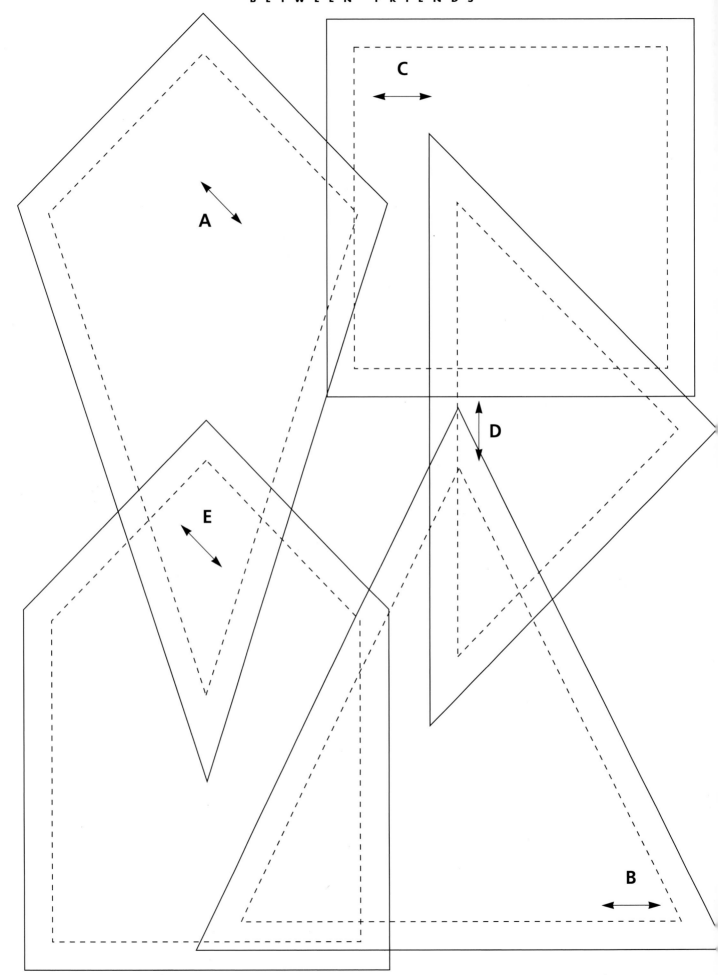

JEWEL OF THE ORIENT

I really love traditional quilts and enjoy experimenting with colour within a traditional framework. I also like simplicity of design. This quilt met all my criteria. With so many willing helpers, the quilt blocks were finished in no time, even though I thought the bright turquoise would mean I would have to supply sunglasses along with the instructions. I am delighted with the finished quilt, which reminds me of a Persian carpet with its glowing colours. The names of my friends in the turquoise squares add the finishing touch.

THESE BLOCKS WERE MADE BY CASTLE HILL FRIENDSHIP QUILTERS, NEW SOUTH WALES, 1990, FOR LYN SHAYLER.

Friendship quilts are always treasured as they are such wonderful reminders of friends and shared moments in our busy lives. In the light of this, I want to thank sincerely the many quilters all over Australia who sent their special quilts to me to be photographed and shared their stories with me. I am very thankful for their trust and their enthusiasm for this book.

As always, the idea of friendship quilts is contagious. At J.B. Fairfax Press the staff has established a friendship group with most of the office involved in making blocks for one another. Two off-site employees (both wives of staff members) participate enthusiastically and one ex-employee waits patiently for her next instructions by mail. It is so exciting to see the latest block arrive at the office. It is also exciting to watch confidence blossom in sewers and non-sewers alike as they learn the intricacies of patchwork and discover the joy of working with fabric. Their enthusiasm has been a wonderful affirmation of all that this book seeks to communicate.

Karen Fail

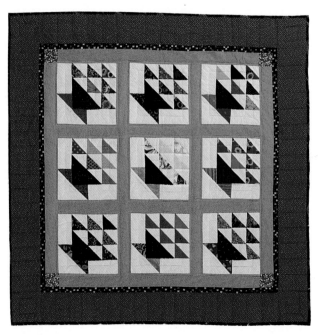

BASKETS OF FRIENDS, *150 cm square, 1995.*
The blocks for this quilt were made by the staff of J.B. Fairfax Press Pty Limited and were won by Judy Poulos in a draw.

EDITORIAL
Managing Editor: Judy Poulos
Editorial Assistant: Ella Martin
Editorial Coordinator: Margaret Kelly
Photography: Andrew Payne
Illustrations: Nicki Rein

DESIGN AND PRODUCTION
Manager: Anna Maguire
Picture Editors: Cheryl Dubyk-Yates,
Stacey Strickland
Production Editor: Sheridan Packer
Concept Design: Michelle Withers

Published by J.B. Fairfax Press Pty Limited
80-82 McLachlan Avenue
Rushcutters Bay, NSW 2011 Australia
A.C.N. 003 738 430

Printed by Toppan Printing Company, Singapore

Copyright J.B. Fairfax Pty Limited 1996

JBFP 445

BETWEEN FRIENDS
Quilts to Share
ISBN 1 86343 278 7

Inside Front and Inside Back Cover: **WASHING DAY,** *164 cm x 204 cm, 1994. Made by the McLaren Vale Quilters for Pam Whaite.*

Classic
Paul Simon:
The Solo Years

A collection of all the music from four landmark Paul Simon albums.
Arranged for piano/vocal with guitar frames and full lyrics.

Amsco Publications
New York/London/Sydney

Order No. PS 11378
US International Standard Book Number: 0.8256.3316.8
UK International Standard Book Number: 0.7119.5151.9

Exclusive Distributors:
Music Sales Corporation
257 Park Avenue South, New York, NY 10010 USA
Music Sales Limited
8/9 Frith Street, London W1V 5TZ England
Music Sales Pty. Limited
120 Rothschild Avenue, Rosebery, Sydney, NSW 2018, Australia

Printed in the United States of America by
Vicks Lithograph and Printing Corporation